Invisible Girls

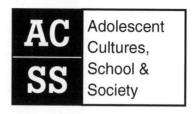

AC / SS — Adolescent Cultures, School & Society

Joseph L. DeVitis & Linda Irwin-DeVitis

GENERAL EDITORS

Vol. 58

This book is part of the Peter Lang Education list.
Every volume is peer reviewed and meets
the highest quality standards for content and production.

PETER LANG
New York • Washington, D.C./Baltimore • Bern
Frankfurt • Berlin • Brussels • Vienna • Oxford

MELLINEE LESLEY

Invisible Girls

At Risk Adolescent
Girls' Writing Within
and Beyond School

PETER LANG
New York • Washington, D.C./Baltimore • Bern
Frankfurt • Berlin • Brussels • Vienna • Oxford

Library of Congress Cataloging-in-Publication Data

Lesley, Mellinee.
Invisible girls: at risk adolescent girls' writing within and beyond school /
Mellinee Lesley.
p. cm. — (Adolescent cultures, school, and society; 58)
Includes bibliographical references and index.
1. Teenage girls—Education—United States. 2. Teenagers with social
disabilities—Education—United States. 3. English language—Composition
and exercises—Study and teaching (Secondary)—United States. 4. Creative
writing (Secondary)—United States. 5. Dropouts—United States—Prevention.
I. Title.
LC1755.L47   373.182352—dc23   2011051544
ISBN 978-1-4331-1494-6 (hardcover)
ISBN 978-1-4331-1493-9 (paperback)
ISBN 978-1-4539-0570-8 (e-book)
ISSN 1091-1464

Bibliographic information published by **Die Deutsche Nationalbibliothek**.
Die Deutsche Nationalbibliothek lists this publication in the "Deutsche
Nationalbibliografie"; detailed bibliographic data is available
on the Internet at http://dnb.d-nb.de/.

For the adolescent girls who graced my life with their stories.

For adolescent girls everywhere.

Table of Contents

Acknowledgments

First, I must acknowledge the Communities in Schools program in the state of Texas. From assisting with the resources needed to purchase glasses to academic tutoring to giving a student a safe place to eat lunch, I have witnessed firsthand the miracles Communities in Schools staff have created in the lives of at-risk youth. Without this program I would never have met the individuals in this book.

I am deeply indebted to the Communities in Schools campus coordinator at the middle school where this study took place. She was my key informant, my support system when a crisis erupted, and my collaborator on many activities. Her calm and optimistic demeanor was a beautiful gift she gave the girls every day.

I am also indebted to the middle school principal who welcomed volunteers into his school to help students and who supported the work I engaged in with the girls.

And I thank Isaac Abrams, who gave permission for his art entitled "All Things Are One" to be reproduced. The timelessness of his work touched the life of a girl from a different generation living on the other side of the Atlantic Ocean.

I must thank my graduate assistant, Heather Kelley, without whose work this book might never have come together. Heather transcribed hundreds of hours of discussion and interviews without complaint. Heather coached the girls on their writing, developed a *MySpace* page for our project, and helped me think through many issues related to gender identity. Heather also baked cupcakes on a regular basis for the writing group and brought gifts to the girls for the slightest occasion.

My profound thanks for this project goes to the brave adolescent girls I worked with at the middle school. Thank you for hanging out with me, giving me the low down about boys, sticking up for one another, and trying almost hopelessly to teach me to be hip. I am a better teacher educator and better human being because of your presence in my life.

Finally, I must acknowledge my family, all of whom encouraged and supported me in unique ways. I thank my mother for instilling in me an unwavering understanding of the importance of education that safeguards human equity and dignity. I thank my father, who inspired me with the power of the written word as a young girl and who continued to advise me about writing in every stage of my life since. I thank my husband for being my first reader and giving up what should have been a relaxing morning in New Mexico to read early drafts of the first three chapters of this book. Thank you for believing in me every step of the way, especially when I was exhausted and depleted emotionally. Thank you for taking time out of your hectic schedule to pick up our children and even cart them to work with you while I disappeared into a Third Space setting. At last, I thank my children, Jonathan and Mireille, the lights of my life, for serving as my litmus test for the rights of all children and for sharing their mommy time, so I could be with adolescent girls they would never meet except in print.

List of Abbreviations

AAUW	American Association of University Women
C.I.S.	Communities in Schools
ICTs	information and communication technologies
IM	instant messaging
I.S.S.	in-school suspension
NAEP	National Assessment of Educational Progress
NCTE	National Council of Teachers of English
TAKS	Texas Assessment of Knowledge and Skills
TANF	Temporary Assistance for Needy Families

Introduction

Four years ago, I began a voluntary writing group with adolescent girls through a program in a middle school designed to provide services to students deemed to be at risk for dropping out of school. My introduction to the girls' writing consisted of brief entries in journals scattered over a few pages and days in the group such as the following examples:

Hi my name is lataydra in I'm here 2 talk about how 2 Get A date with your daddy 1st you have 2 see how he's going.

My day was good I guess you can say. I got to see my boyfriend since he was absent yesterday. I got to see my friends also, they always have alot to say Now I'm here writing in this journal. Not knowing what to say. I thought today was going to be bad, but I guess it didn't. I'm glad that it didn't. So I guess I'll stop writing, so good-bye.

Today was a BORING day.

I see that Angelica doesn't know how to comb her hair it on the top of her head looks like she just got out of bed.

Today was FUN because in PE we played hooky.

As time goes by I see the past
I swish throu the sky as my grandma says good bye.
I turn to the side and wish she was still alive.
I cry to sleep asking why lord why.
Why did she have to say goodbye.

Today was boring the only time I have fun is in 1st and 3rd period.

Today wuz good I just did my work and talk to my friend it wuz a normal day then I was thinking about Joe.

Today my day was boring. I didn't like my day very much. I was writing alot of notes to my friends through Kecia gets on my nerves too.

When I see my mother cry I get sad and I feel guilt in me because I feel like I have done something but I know that she is just crying because she has been through alot!

Today so born because in luch we had to seat where had put us but it was fun at the table I seat in.

One day at church my "boyfriend" Chris got arested for clowning on the cop it was so funny.

Each entry offered a poignant glimpse into the girls' daily realities with school, peers, boys, and family. Through observing them as writers, I also learned about the kinds of support sixth, seventh, and eighth grade at-risk girls needed in order to produce written text. Most notably, I came to view "best practices" for writing instruction with these students as possessing a unique place within the conceptual grounding of writing process pedagogy for adolescents (e.g., Atwell, 1998; Elbow, 1973; Kittle, 2008; Rief, 2007; Zemelman & Daniels, 1988). Moreover, constructing the project as a Third Space[1] writing group—located in the school but remaining separate from the routines, curriculum, and evaluative processes of the school—created a conduit between the realms of out-of-school and in-school writing practices the girls experienced. In this manner, the Third Space setting made visible certain important factors that place girls at risk for academic failure and ways writing pedagogy can serve to alter the trajectory of high school attrition looming before them.

At the conclusion of her book *Just Girls: Hidden Literacies and Life in Junior High*, Finders (1997) wrote of the importance of literacy instruction for adolescent girls:

> Left to their own devices, students have few options but to live out received scripts, invisible and impossible to révise. Literacy instruction can begin to make visible to students the roles that are presently available in our texts, in our classrooms, in our society. When we begin to examine the motivations behind particular publications, we begin to change those publications. (pp. 130–131)

A decade later, literacy instruction concerned with fostering positive identities for adolescent girls is still critical (Archer, Halsall, & Hollingworth, 2007). A recent American Association of University Women (AAUW) study, "Where the Girls Are: The Facts About Gender Equity in Education" (2008), revealed that adolescent girls in the United States most at risk for dropping out of high school and otherwise falling through the cracks of academic achievement are ethnic minority girls from low-income families. Noting similar concerns, Inness (2000) wrote in the preface to *Running for Their Lives: Girls, Cultural Identity, and Stories of Survival*:

---

[1] Third Space theory is discussed in Chapter One.

> For many reasons all the world's girls are placed in the margins of existence. But how much infinitely more complex and perilous this situation is when girls are doubly or triply marginalized by socioeconomic class, race, ethnicity, and a host of other factors. (p. xi)

The demographic point where gender, minority status, and low family income converge places girls in a precarious position for obtaining a high school diploma, meeting the passing requirements of state mandated standardized tests, and being admitted into institutions of higher education.

In her study of a high school teacher working to empower ethnic minority adolescents through writing, Fisher (2007) noted,

> All too often there is an assumption in the education community that promoting student self-awareness through writing and performance means that students are not acquiring the skills they need for "academic literacy." In the 21st century, the traditional English teacher has to be so much more; he or she also has to be a healer. This is especially true in urban public schools. (p. 14)

To build on Fisher's ideas of contemporary writing pedagogy and address the needs of ethnic minority girls from low-income families that the AAUW report illuminated, I conducted a three-and-a-half-year study with this population of learners considered most at risk for not achieving academic success in order to gain a sense of: (1) Who are at-risk girls? (2) What role does writing play in their lives? And, (3) What can schools do to prevent the loss of their intellectual potential? Through such questions, I hoped to find a way to help at-risk girls use writing to "aspire beyond 'ascribed lives'" (Fisher, 2007, p. 19).

In analyzing the writing produced in the group, I soon realized my inquiry not only pertained to print the girls composed but also textual elements extending beyond print that were similarly used to produce and sustain narratives about the girls' identities (e.g., spoken Discourse, music, multimodal media, photos, symbols). I also discovered all writing created by the girls was driven by an underlying autobiographical impulse. In fact, to a large extent, my work highlighted the intricate and mirroring relationship between self and text for these adolescent girls who used writing as an emotional salve and social subterfuge in order to sort through their life experiences, self-actualize, practice gender roles, and document their slow but methodical disengagement from school. On a good day Amber wrote in a piece she entitled "Feeling Krunk":

> But all people think
> I'm a ghetto girl from the hood, but I know I'm
> not just that I'm more than that. I'm a smart,
> strong minded girl with goals and future. I

know this might be what some people say and
it never happens. Because they might get all
strung out but I know that isn't going to [be] me.

On a bad day, Amber wrote about struggling with memories of being molested when she was five, boys constantly calling her fat in school, and contemplating "ending it all."

If writing skills are a key measure to academic success and writing is one of the few places at-risk adolescent girls have to give voice to their life experiences, then writing pedagogy for this population of learners is critical and much more care needs to be given to their literacy practices and pedagogical needs. Consequently, the purpose for this book is to offer educators resources for teaching writing to the considerable number of adolescent girls who are struggling unnoticed in classrooms and invisibly being failed by the public education system in the United States.

References

American Association of University Women. (2008). *Where the girls are: The facts about gender equity in education.* Washington, DC: Author.

Archer, L., Halsall, A., & Hollingworth, S. (2007). Inner-city feminities and education: "Race," class, gender and schooling in young women's lives. *Gender and Education, 19* (5), 549–568.

Atwell, N. (1998). *In the middle: New understandings about writing, reading, and learning.* Portsmouth, NH: Boynton/Cook.

Elbow, P. (1973). *Writing without teachers.* New York: Oxford University Press.

Finders, M. (1997). *Just girls: Hidden literacies and life in junior high.* New York: Teachers College Press.

———. (2007). *Writing in rhythm: Spoken word poetry in urban classrooms.* New York: Teachers College Press.

Inness, S. (2000). *Running for their lives: Girls, cultural identity, and stories of survival.* Lanham, MD: Rowman & Littlefield.

Kittle, P. (2008). *Write beside them: Risk, voice, and clarity in high school writing.* Portsmouth, NH: Heinemann.

Rief, L. (2007). Writing commonsense matters. In K. Beers, R. Probst, and L. Rief (Eds.), *Adolescent literacy: Turning promise into practice.* (pp. 189–212). Portsmouth, NH: Heinemann.

Zemelman, S., & Daniels, H. (1988). *A community of writers: Teaching writing in the junior and senior high.* Portsmouth, NH: Heinemann.

Chapter One

"In Middle School, You Like Do the Most Growing Up": Exploring Writing with Adolescent Girls

My Narrative

The impetus for this book began nearly two decades ago when I was hired to teach English at a private, Catholic high school for girls in El Paso, Texas. The president of the school at this time, Sister Helen, often stated in faculty meetings that all of us were part of the faculty to fulfill a higher purpose. When she made statements such as this, she would pause and look carefully around the room to lock eyes with the elliptical configuration of partially attentive teachers. This discursive gesture drawn out for dramatic effect was to intimate that our presence in the school was part of a divine path, a calling of sorts. As a new teacher, I was not convinced Sister Helen was speaking to me. In fact, as a new teacher I felt like an awkward inter-loper in nearly every step I took beyond my classroom door. Even so, the years I spent teaching in this context shaped much of my subsequent work in the field of literacy education.

While teaching at this school, I experienced a powerful lesson of what happens to girls in an educational setting where the major distinctions of gender (i.e., male and female dominant and submissive roles) are stripped away. With no male peers in the setting, the girls were free to express ideas without gender-induced inhibition and outmoded notions of making a choice between being pretty or being smart. They were free to rise intellectually. In fact, part of the school's curriculum entailed teaching the girls that they could achieve any professional and academic goal they so desired. As such, a major facet to the mission of the school was to secure admission at the best universities in the nation with competitive academic scholarships for all students upon graduation from high school.

As a new teacher, I entered into a curriculum that was predicated upon the now famous American Association of University Women (AAUW) report "How Schools Short Change Girls" (1992). This report was the subject of much professional development and faculty meeting discussions. Texts read in ninth grade English were selected on the basis of the presence of a female protagonist. The school routinely had guest speakers who were successful female judges, newscasters, doctors, lawyers, professors, and businesswomen. A product of a small, public school in rural Iowa, as I sought to educate students in this setting, so was I equally educated about the potential deprived of adolescent females by limited and unexamined notions of gender roles. When I watched girls at this school stand up and give speeches with confidence to the entire student body, vigorously discuss a host of derogatory terms for females they were exposed to on a daily basis, and write award-winning essays about their future aspirations, I was filled with questions about gender and literacy that hinged on some elusive intersection of language, text, and feminist agency. Inspired by the burgeoning academic potential of the students, I left teaching high school to pursue a Ph.D. in literacy education where I could explore theories that addressed my questions about the unique circumstances gender creates for literacy development with adolescents.

After completing a doctorate, I continued my journey as a teacher educator and literacy practitioner through working with marginalized (Moje, 2000) populations of learners. Such contexts entailed teaching adult basic education classes, tutoring "struggling" students in an alternative high school in a rural community, teaching at-risk high school students in an urban community, and teaching developmental readers at a state university. Gender issues in all of these settings cropped up most visibly in the form of female students contending with sexual abuse and childcare needs. Female students dotting the margins of these educational settings were often trying to overcome a myriad of social obstacles in order to complete a high school education or successfully navigate college coursework.

Following several years of teaching between the cracks of high school and college, I realized how truly privileged my former high school students were due to the fact they had experienced a space in their education as adolescents in which their voices as individual girls and a collective of females were *cultivated*. Gender was not an obstacle to be overcome; rather, it was a resource from which to draw personal insights, purpose, and perseverance. Although I did not believe it at the time, Sister Helen was right. There was a reason for my presence in the all-girls high school that extended far beyond teaching *The Scarlet Letter*. I, too, was privileged to be part of a rare form of schooling for adolescent girls. Perhaps most important, the girls at this school created a point of comparison from which I could measure the schooling experiences of other adolescent girls I subsequently encountered struggling through the thoroughly trodden scripts of gender roles in educational settings.

The other impetus for this study came from my recent work with a small group of "at-risk" high school students in a Communities in Schools–sponsored literacy project (Lesley, 2008; Lesley, 2009). In this setting I worked with both male and female ethnically diverse students. While all of the students in this project had been identified as at risk, the girls were in a uniquely precarious position as learners. In a span of three semesters, I lost two girls from the small group due to pregnancy. One of the girls was sixteen, mildly mentally retarded, and living with her boyfriend, who had been seen hitting her in the school's cafeteria. This student moved with her mother to another city to escape her abusive boyfriend and give birth to her baby. The other girl was seventeen, an honors student, and completely homebound once her baby was born in November of her senior year. I also lost a girl from the literacy project due to the fact she had to travel home every day at noon to prepare lunch for her father. Because she often did not return to school in the afternoon, her attendance at school was greatly hampered by her family's gender role expectations. The remaining girls who participated in the literacy project were perpetually sullen, emotionally volatile, and just plain angry about their perceived constant battle with social victimization in the school (e.g., struggling with deceptive friendships and fights, making the pom squad, dealing with sexual harassment, finding a homecoming or prom dress in spite of their family's poverty.)

As I have continued to work with numerous marginalized populations of learners, I have become aware of the unique ways gender (especially when coupled with poverty) places adolescent girls at risk for academic failure and have become interested in the role literacy can play in the lives of adolescent girls as a means through which to examine and redress such disparities. I have also become intrigued by the ways at-risk adolescent girls use literacy—more specifically, narratives—to replicate, submerge, and transform their identities. From such queries, I constructed the writing group for middle school girls to gain a deeper understanding of the manner in which gender plays out in at-risk adolescent girls' writing.

Context for the Writing Group

I initiated the writing group with students attending an urban middle school located in a Texas city in the United States.[1] Nestled on the edge of an aging, middle-class community, the school in which I conducted the study resided two blocks away from one of the main thoroughfares in the city. A year prior to the beginning of the study, the demographics of the student body shifted as an influx of low-income families moved into apartments and small homes located in proximity to the school. The Communities in Schools (C.I.S.) coordinator at the middle school explained the shift was the result of a low-income neighborhood several streets away being gentrified to make way for high-rise condominiums, hip coffee shops, national restaurant chains, and trendy boutiques. In a preliminary interview, the C.I.S. coordinator also noted the influx of low-income students had raised the school's free and reduced lunch rate and lowered the school's state mandated standardized test scores.

At the beginning of the study, the school's percentage of students classified as economically disadvantaged was seventy-eight percent. At the conclusion of the study this percentage had risen slightly to eighty percent. For purposes of comparison, the state average for economically disadvantaged students in a single middle school is fifty-five percent. The last year of the study, the school had less than one percent of gifted and talented students. Comparatively, the state average for gifted and talented students in middle school is eight percent. Similarly, the school had twenty-seven percent special education students compared to the state average of ten percent. Sixty-three percent of the students were Hispanic, twenty-one percent of the students were white, and fifteen percent of the students were African American. At the beginning of the study the school had an "academically unacceptable" rating—the lowest rating possible in the state ranking system based on passing rates of standardized test scores. By the conclusion of the study, the school had raised its test scores to move up one rung to an "academically acceptable" ranking. A year following the study, the school dipped back down to an unacceptable rating. The C.I.S. coordinator correlated the dip in academic ranking with the influx of students possessing new backgrounds and needs the school personnel were not prepared to handle. I credited a great deal of the improvement in ranking over the three-and-a-half years of the study to the school hiring an energetic and pedagogically focused principal.

---

[1] Please see Appendix A for a description of the research methodology I employed to gather and analyze data in this setting.

Even with the school's improvement in standardized test scores during the project, girls at the school lagged behind their male counterparts in nearly every subject at nearly every grade level. The last year of the study, sixth grade girls scored six percentage points below their male counterparts in reading and seventeen percentage points below them in mathematics. Seventh grade girls scored seven percentage points below boys in reading, one percentage point above boys in writing, and twelve percentage points below boys in mathematics. In eighth grade, girls scored three points above boys in reading, one point below boys in social studies, five points below boys in science, and one point below boys in mathematics.

For three-and-a-half years, I worked with the adolescent girls who contributed to these test scores in an after school and during school writing group. Through this project, I engaged in weekly dialogues and writing activities with the girls attending this ethnically diverse middle school swelling with a higher than average number of new teachers and veteran teachers adjusting to new student demographics. The writing group was organized through a community volunteer project sponsored by the Communities in Schools program. C.I.S. is the largest federally funded drop-out prevention program in the United States. The participants in this setting consisted of sixth, seventh, and eighth grade girls registered with the C.I.S. program. Students are recruited to participate in the C.I.S. program based on their probability for dropping out of high school. These risk factors consist of students who: have failed two or more classes, have not been promoted to the next grade level, are pregnant or teen parents, are homeless, are eligible for free lunch, are TANF (Temporary Assistance for Needy Families) eligible, have failed the Texas Assessment of Knowledge and Skills (TAKS) test, are on probation, are currently in a family crisis, or have an incarcerated parent.

I approached the project from the philosophy of Third Space. Moje et. al. (2004) described Third Space as "the integration of knowledges and Discourses drawn from . . . the 'first space' of people's home, community, and peer networks with the 'second space' of the Discourses they encounter in more formalized institutions such as work, school, or church" (p. 41). Gutierrez (2008) described Third Space as a place "in which students begin to reconceive who they are and what they might be able to accomplish academically and beyond" (p. 148). Cook (2005) defined Third Space around three tenets: "the use of 'funds of knowledge,' the support for home-type discourse and the explicit connection of this with teaching for the production of 'schooled' texts" (p. 87). In constructing the writing group as a Third Space, I sought to help students build on their school literacies through their use of out-of-school literacies. I also sought to support the girls' development of agentive literacy identities in both school and out-of-school settings for writing.

In the beginning of this study, I tried to direct writing activities with the girls through various prompts and suggested formats for writing. After a year of trial and error with various writing techniques, some more successful than others, I restructured my approach to allow the girls complete autonomy with writing. Initially, I worked with a colleague to develop weekly group sessions that followed a structure of: (1) snack time, (2) freewriting in journals for ten minutes, (3) a minilesson about writing or a reading activity, (4) a writing activity connected to the minilesson or reading, and (5) time for sharing and commenting on one another's writing. This format yielded a great deal of tension among the girls. Towards the end of the first semester, the girls simply refused to write in their journals, talked during the minilesson, and paid minimal attention at best to each other's writing. Instead of support and feedback, the girls often made snide remarks towards one another, which occasionally escalated into tears and fights. Upon reflection, I realized this approach was too reminiscent of the hierarchies of a school setting where "good" readers and writers are revered and unsuccessful bullies are cultivated. By the third session of the weekly writing group, the girls' waning interest for this format as well as the ways they responded positively to individual interactions with me were already evident.

One day during this time frame in the project, as the girls were arriving to the group, Demetria handed me a poem she had written. I read it and told her how good I thought it was. Demetria beamed with pride. Overhearing our exchange, Savannah showed me a poem she had written about bubble gum for a class. I read this poem enthusiastically too and asked the few girls who were listening if they thought we should do some poetry writing in our group. They all responded positively. When we began journal writing, Demetria pulled out her poem and recopied it into her journal verbatim. Most of the other girls, however, did not write. Tara and Lataydra continued to talk during the entire freewriting time. When the ten minutes for journal writing was up, Tara declared she had nothing to write about since she spent the day in I.S.S. (in-school suspension) staring at a blackboard. I told her to repeat what she had just said. She did so somewhat hesitantly. Then, I asked the rest of the girls if Tara's words conjured up an image in their mind of what she did. They all said, "Yes." I asked them to think back to the poetry we had read the week before and how I had asked them if it conjured up images and feelings for them. "So," I continued, "Tara's words are like the poems. If she writes them down they will be poetry." Turning back to Tara, I said, "Write down what you just said in your journal and put today's date." With several doubtful looks towards me, she wrote the words in her journal reluctantly, as if her pencil was moving through a layer of sludge.

After two semesters of tepid results and my colleague resigning from the project in frustration over the girls' torpid attitudes towards writing, I decided to restructure my approach to writing instruction to one of giving the girls complete autonomy with their writing during the group. Instead of the format described above, I took the girls to a cluster of computers in the library and encouraged them to write by asking them simply, "What do you want to write about today?" This shift in the group's structure to more individualized work and autonomy with writing topics and formats necessitated a shift in my role as well from one of writing teacher to that of writing mentor.

During the three-and-a-half years of the study, the group fluctuated in membership as girls moved from the school, encountered scheduling conflicts, lost interest in participating, or advanced to high school. Even with such fluctuations, by the conclusion of the study, I had collected data over twenty-four sixth, seventh, and eighth grade girls, eight of whom I was able to follow for two years and seven of whom I was able to follow for three years. The girls ranged in their academic aptitude from one participant who had Down's syndrome and was receiving full services in special education to several participants who were taking pre-AP classes. At the beginning of the study when I was attempting to direct writing instruction, I focused on free-writing in journals and formulas for writing poetry (e.g., found poetry, looking at lyrics of pop songs by Chris Brown as poetry) because several of the girls had expressed interest in writing poetry outside of school on their own time. During this phase of the project, I also gathered several samples of elaborate and subversively written notes composed by the girls for their peers. Some of these notes contained poetry as well. Even in an age where nearly all of the girls had *MySpace* accounts (an online social networking site), several had text messaging capabilities on their cell phones, and access to instant messenger via the school's electronic networking system, this seemingly anachronistic writing practice was still a valued form of writing in classroom settings where access to such technology was prohibited. At the conclusion of the first phase of the study, I created a booklet of the girls' writing and invited them to compose texts they wanted included in the booklet electronically. This publishing process helped to solidify the purpose of the group.

In the second year of the study, I met after school with the girls in a classroom reserved for use by the C.I.S. campus coordinator. I also incorporated reading two books with the ongoing writing taking place each week,

Who Am I Without Him? (Flake, 2004) and *Chicken Soup for the Teen Soul* (Canfield, Hansen, & Kirberger, 1997). During this period of time, students engaged in primarily prompted discussion and writing in response to readings from these texts. The format of this approach yielded mixed results in terms of the interest levels of the students with respect to participating in the group. The readings spawned rich discussions about parents, peers, bullies, school structures, and boys as well as revealed particular patterns in Discourse (Gee, 2005) and configurations of cliques among the girls. The readings did not generate increased interest in writing, however. Halfway through this year, I engaged in less reading and shifted the focus to unprompted composing of texts on computers.

At the beginning of the final year and a half of the study, I received permission from the school's principal to meet with the girls during their advisory period in the library where we could use several computers with limited Internet access. Meeting in the middle of the school day permitted girls to attend the group who were busy with competitive athletics practice after school. Even though I had changed the setting, I continued to approach writing as a completely self-directed activity. This method allowed the girls to experiment with multiple genres of text and formats facilitated by a digital medium (e.g., power point slides and downloaded photographs). Being of the same gender but from an entirely different generation, higher socioeconomic class, and a different race from most of the girls in the writing group created subtle obstacles of trust that took time to overcome. It took time for the girls to trust me to read their real writing and confide in me. The girls perpetually interviewed me about my life, my family, my job, and my income. After they felt they could trust me, they began to share secrets about friendships, dating, and traumatic experiences with me in their writing and discussions. Then, they began to seek my advice about writing. Once they knew they could write any way about any topic without being judged by this older, white, teacher-like person, they not only wrote about more intellectually complex topics, but they also began to take greater care with the mechanics of their writing and deepen their sense of writing to an audience.

The National Focus on Adolescent Literacy

The framework for this book is grounded in recent studies involving adolescents' literacy practices. Engagement and success in literacy tasks for adolescents is a growing area of research in the field of literacy education (Ippolito, Steele, & Samson, 2008; Jacobs, 2008; Moje, Overby, Tysvaer, & Morris, 2008; see also Faggella-Luby, Ware, & Capozzoli, 2009). The *NCTE Policy Research Brief on Adolescent Literacy* (2007) by the National Council of Teachers of English begins with causes for concern about adolescent literacy based on recent studies and NAEP (National Assessment of Educational Progress) data. Citing NAEP data on adolescent writing skills, the Policy Research Brief states: "40 percent of high school seniors never or rarely write a paper of three or more pages, and although 4th and 8th graders showed some improvement in writing between 1998 and 2002, the scores of 12th graders showed no significant gain" (Retrieved October 5, 2010, from http://www.org/library/NCTEFiles/Resources/PolicyResearchAdolLitResear ch Brief.pdf). Similarly, several studies have noted the problem of adolescents' lack of motivation towards engaging in school forms of literacy (Mahiri, 2004; Moje, 2000; Guzzetti & Gamboa, 2004; Reed, Schallert, Beth, & Woodruff, 2004) as well as the imperative for teachers to embrace theories of adolescent literacy to combat this problem (e.g., Rycik & Irvin, 2001). From Frost's (2001) account of creating a "safe" environment for students to write about traumatic experiences to Reynold's (2004) work with reaching reluctant teen readers to Hutchinson's (1999) research on the ways teachers' narratives supplant students' narratives in high school classroom environments, the field of literacy education is developing a growing body of knowledge focused on the dignity and marginalization of adolescents' experiences with literacy in school settings.

In some of the research on adolescent literacy, specific concern has been raised over adolescent girls and the unique social and academic challenges they face with respect to literacy engagement, membership in Discourse communities, and resistance to gender stereotypes (e.g., Hubbard, Barbieri, & Power, 1998; see also Pipher, 1994). Guzzetti and Gamboa's (2004) research, for instance, examined the phenomenon of middle- to upper-middle-class European American adolescent girls' publication of 'zines—magazine-type publications—the adolescent girls in their study created as a way to "talk back" to layers of social norms they felt confronted by as feminists, anarchists, and activists. Membership is such Discourse communities gave rise to the zines, which were constructed around critiques of popular culture. Finders (1997) also noted the "literate underlife" of early adolescent girls as a way to understand, resist, and foster socially defined roles for females (p. 1). In her ethnography of seventh grade girls, Finders investigated the role social configurations played in adolescent girls' literacy practices. In particular, she theorized that for adolescent girls, "one's membership within groups regulates literate practices" and can serve to impede intellectual mobility (p. 5). Similarly, she noted "social roles" were "defined and constrained by text" both consumed and produced by the girls in her study (p. 5).

Hubbard, Barbieri, and Power (1998) captured the complexity of adolescent girls' literacies in finding a common denominator that is largely delineated by the pervasive silencing of adolescent girls through social norms and school identities. Even so, Hubbard, Barbieri, and Power highlighted the fact that while so much of adolescent girls' literacies are hidden and silenced, adolescent girls nonetheless "want to be known" and want their lives to matter in broader society. This struggle between hidden texts and public roles was replicated in the narrative identities the adolescent girls in their book presented.

Since the AAUW report "How Schools Short Change Girls" was published in 1992, increased attention has been given to issues of gender equity in educational settings. In a recent follow-up study by the AAUW, "Where the Girls Are: The Facts about Gender Equity in Education (2008), new research has indicated that "disparities by race/ethnicity and family income level" play a stronger role in determining equity for girls than was previously believed (p. xi). Looking at statistical data since 1970 from NAEP, SAT, and ACT test scores, the report stated:

> Gender differences in educational achievement vary by race/ethnicity and family income level. For example, girls often have outperformed boys within each racial/ethnic group on the NAEP reading test. When broken down by race/ethnicity, however, this gender gap is found to be most consistent among white students, less so among African American students, and least among Hispanic students. Similarly, boys overall have outperformed girls on both the math and verbal portions of the SAT. Disaggregated by family income level, however, the male advantage on the verbal portion of the SAT is consistently seen only among students from low-income families. (p. 3)

According to this statistical analysis, equity in gender achievement is most concerning for minority status girls from low-income families, the very girls who participated in the writing group.

Even with the increased attention on adolescent literacy, more needs to be known about the literacy practices of adolescent girls. In particular, more attention needs to be given to the unique challenges intersections of gender, peer groups, ethnicity, academic performance, and socio-economic status create for adolescent girls. Given that literacy skills are a key element for academic success for all learners, understanding literacy development vis-à-vis gender identity for at-risk adolescent girls is crucial in order to be able to close this current gender gap, which the AAUW has deemed to require urgent action (p. 4).

The Role of Identity and Agency in Adolescents' Literacy Development

Identity plays a key role in addressing adolescent girls' literacies. Gee (2005) sifted through the complexity of human subjectivities to define identity as "different ways of participating in different social groups, cultures, and institutions" (p. 1). He explained such participation in social groups is "a nearly endless ever-changing list" (p. 1). In Gee's model of identity, the symbolic action and participation in various forms of Discourse invite individuals to identify with an assortment of social groups. Similarly, Hall (2004) referred to discourses and their attendant practices as the points through which identities are "sutured" to an individual (p. 19). Hall stated:

> Precisely because identities are constructed within, not outside discourses, we need to understand them as produced in specific historical and institutional sites within specific discursive formations and practices by specific enunciative strategies. (p. 17)

In addition to the role of Discourse in forming identities, Hall wrote of the inborn power structures attached to identities. Hall cautioned that identities "emerge within the specific modalities of power, and thus are more the product of the marking of difference and exclusion" (p. 17). Building onto Hall's observation of the degrees of social capital inherent in Discourse and identities, Skeggs (2008) noted identities are not "equally available to all" and embody hierarchies of power (p. 11). In this manner, identity is tightly knit to agency.

Research predicated upon a view of literacy as a form of personal and collective agency has been spawned from both socio-cultural theories of language studies (e.g., Ahearn, 2001; Heath, 2004) and theories of critical literacy (e.g., Freire, 1995). Feminist approaches to critical literacy have been similarly concerned with the ways language is used to both silence females and ascribe authority over them based on gendered divisions in educational settings (Lewis, 1993; Luke & Gore, 1992). Because each of these theoretical domains views language as a form of symbolic action, language use is deemed to be tantamount to social behavior. Critical literacy and feminist research in particular compelled the study of language as social action forward through an examination of multiple viewpoints and whose perspectives are given authority over others. As such, critical literacy and feminist research have been deeply concerned with the role of agency in creating contexts for literacy that seek to redress social inequities.

With respect to the field of adolescent literacy, Moore and Cunningham (2006) defined literacy agency for adolescents as "self direction" imparting a view of agency as action (p. 129). They set this definition in opposition to external reading reform efforts that seek to control adolescent literacy through defining reading and writing as passive endeavors. As part of viewing agency in literacy as an active stance, Moore and Cunningham situated literacy agency within an understanding of agency as connected to identity and considered "adolescents' agency relative to their academic reading and writing" identities (p. 130).

In tandem to the research examining literacy as agency, a great deal has been written about adolescents' literacy identities as a basis for reading engagement (Alvermann & Heron, 2001; DeBlase, 2003; Lenters, 2006). Williams (2006) explained the role of literacy identity with respect to adolescents' reading behavior from the perspective of classroom teachers:

> When we teach reading, we want students to do more than simply comprehend the words on the page; we want them to investigate and interpret the work. Whether it be a poem, novel, or essay, we would like to see students invest themselves in their reading—to see them connect their ideas and their experiences with the words on the page. (p. 149)

Along with such views of engaged reading identities as agentive in nature, literacy researchers have also theorized that resistant literacy identities are a form of agency as well (Lenters, 2006). Moore and Cunningham (2006) explained: "Students choose to identify themselves as rebels because they believe traditional school practices represent corrupt race-, class-, or gender-based power structures or because they consider these practices irrelevant to their current concerns and future aspirations" (p. 141).

Whether a student presents a resistant or engaged stance, Hull and Katz (2006) argued that agency is closely tied to narratives and one's sense of identity as a "storied self" (p. 46). In this manner, autobiographical narratives offer a venue for developing agency, which is reflective of one's identities. Hull and Katz cited Bruner's (1994) notion of "turning points" in autobiography to explain the ways agency is forged through narrative. "Turning points" are moments when individuals report a dramatic change in their life and sense of self; a point at which they become agentive in the way they represent themselves to others (Hull & Katz, p. 45). In this manner narrative agency is closely tied to one's literacy identity (DeBlase, 2003).

The crux of agency in adolescents' literacy identities has to do with the ways students form literacy identities. Alvermann (2001) wrote of the formation of student literacy identities, "Often our identities as readers are decided for us, as when others label us as avid readers, slow readers, mystery readers, and the like. By taking up one or more of these identities, we soon learn to recognize ourselves and others who are like us" (p. 676). Alvermann's point is especially important to consider in light of this study given the fact that nearly all of the girls had been previously labeled as struggling readers and writers and academically at-risk students. Also, much of the girls' identities as writers were carefully locked away in a hidden Discourse with a limited audience.

Concluding Vignette: Beginning Questions

One afternoon a few weeks into the formation of the writing group, Tara ran to get a textbook from her English class to show me a poem entitled "Dreams" by Langston Hughes that her class had read earlier that day. Even though she appeared slightly flustered as she stumbled through reading the text aloud, the poem had touched something in her that she wanted me to see and share with her.

> "Dreams"
> Hold fast to dreams
> For if dreams die
> Life is a broken-winged bird
> That cannot fly.
> Hold fast to dreams
> For when dreams go
> Life is a barren field
> Frozen with snow.

After Tara finished reading the poem Samantha showed up with two friends who were not in the writing group. Tara read another poem from the literature textbook. Then, Samantha fished out three poems from her back-pack that a friend (not present) had written dealing with advice about boys. Once the topic of boys was introduced into conversation, Samantha's friends took charge of the dialogue by making jokes about which girls were and were not virgins at the school. They told stories about a twelve-year-old girl who had a "tiny" baby and another twelve-year-old girl who had "unpro-tected sex" twice with a sixteen-year-old boy and was afraid she was going to get pregnant. I spent most of the time in this discussion fighting a sense of panic while listening and trying to ascertain whether or not the girls were exaggerating these stories for my benefit. Were they testing me or confiding in me? At one point Tara asserted that she was not a virgin, went into elaborate detail about how she routinely played "hooky" from school to have sex with another sixth grade boy in her neighborhood, but then tacked on the words "just kidding" after the conclusion of her narrative. While I felt very disturbed by the discussion of sixth grade virginity among the small group of girls casually tossing words around a table in the library and was unsure about who was bragging and who was telling the truth, I left this session thinking that the social lives of sixth grade girls had become very compli-cated. I also left the session wondering about my role as an adult mentor in the group and questioning what writing had to do with the girls' experiences inside and outside of school. How did we go so quickly from Langston Hughes's "Dreams" to a narrative about a twelve-year-old-girl having unprotected sex with a sixteen-year-old boy? Was this in fact an example of the schism in realities between school and home or between First Space and Second Space settings the girls had to navigate?

As I reflect now over the work I have put into this project and after hav-ing just said another apprehensive goodbye to the last four girls in the writing group to leave eighth grade, I think about the questions I have pondered from the beginning of the study to the conclusion. While I have wondered about many facets of our work together, such as my role as a writing teacher, the literacy practices of the girls outside of school, and the ways the girls used language to assert public and private authority, the question I keep returning to is a larger question of the relative anonymity of these girls in American society. Who knows about the numbers of at-risk girls floundering in schools across the United States? Why are schools not meeting the educational needs of these students? What is the connection between the girls' literacy practices both in school and out of school and their risk for dropping out of school? How can teacher education programs better prepare teachers to work with at-risk girls? Given the paucity of intervention programs targeting at-risk girls, how much do we ultimately care about these girls as a society?

While I continue to be haunted by many of these questions, through my exploration I have been able to develop an understanding of the kinds of writing instruction at-risk girls need in order to develop agentive literacy identities and writing skills expected in academic settings. And, perhaps ultimately if we can construct writing pedagogy that will strengthen at-risk girls, we will be able to accomplish Finders's (1997) goal of creating literacy pedagogy that fosters justice for all adolescent girls.

References

American Association of University Women. (1992). How schools short change girls: Action guide, strategies for improving gender equity in schools. Washington, DC: Author.

————. (2008). Where the girls are: The facts about gender equity in education. Washington, DC: Author.

Ahearn, L. (2001). Language and agency. *Annual Review of Anthropology*, *30*, 109–137.

Alvermann, D. (2001). Reading adolescents' reading identities: Looking back to see ahead. *Journal of Adolescent & Adult Literacy*, 44 (8), 676–690.

Alvermann, D., & Heron, A. (2001). Literacy identity work: Playing to learn with popular media. *Journal of Adolescent & Adult Literacy*, *45* (2), 118–122.

Canfield, J., Hansen, M., & Kirberger, K. (1997). *Chicken soup for the teenage soul: 101 stories of life, love and learning.* Deerfield Beach, FL: Health Communications Incorporated.

Cook, M. (2005). "A place of their own": Creating a classroom "third space" to support a continuum of text construction between home and school. *Literacy*, *9* (2), 85–90.

DeBlase, G. (2003). Acknowledging agency while accommodating romance: Girls negotiating meaning in literacy transactions. *Journal of Adolescent & Adult Literacy*, 46 (8), 624635.

Faggella-Luby, M., Ware, S., & Capozzoli, A. (2009). Adolescent literacy—reviewing adolescent literacy reports: Key components and critical questions. *Journal of Literacy Research*, *41*, 453–475.

Finders, M. (1997). *Just girls: Hidden literacies and life in junior high.* New York: Teachers College Press.

Flake, S. (2004). *Who am I without him? Short stories about girls and the boys in their lives.* New York: Hyperion Books.

Freire, P. (1995). *Pedagogy of hope: Reliving pedagogy of the oppressed.* New York: Continuum.

Frost, H. (2001). *When I whisper, nobody listens: Helping young people write about difficult issues.* Portsmouth, NH: Heinemann.

Gee, J. (2005). *An introduction to discourse analysis theory and method.* New York: Routledge.

Gutierrez, K. (2008). Developing a sociocritical literacy in the third space. *Reading Research Quarterly*, *43* (2) 148–164.

Guzzetti, B., & Gamboa, M. (2004). Zines for social justice: Adolescent girls writing on their own. *Reading Research Quarterly*, *39* (4), 408–436.

Hall, S. (2004). Who needs "identity"? In P. Du Gay, J. Evans, and P. Redman (Eds.), *Identity: A reader.* (pp. 15–30). London: Sage Publications.

Heath, S. B. (2004). The children of trackton's children: Spoken and written language in social change. In R. Ruddell and N. Unrau (Eds.), *Theoretical models and processes of reading.* (pp. 187–209). Newark, DE; International Reading Association.

Hubbard, R., Barbieri, M., & Power, B. (1998). *"We want to be known": Learning from adolescent girls.* York, ME: Stenhouse.

Hull, G., & Katz, M. (2006). Crafting an agentive self: Case studies of digital storytelling. *Research in the Teaching of English*, *41* (1), 43–81.

Hutchinson, J. (1999). *Students on the margins: Education, stories, dignity.* Albany, NY: State University of New York Press.

Ippolito, J., Steele, J., & Samson, J. (2008). Introduction: Why adolescent literacy matters now? *Harvard Educational Review*, *78* (1), 1–6.

Jacobs, V. (2008). Adolescent literacy: Putting the crisis in context. *Harvard Educational Review, 78* (1), 7–39.

Lenters, K. (2006). Resistance, struggle, and the adolescent reader. *Journal of Adolescent & Adult Literacy, 50* (2), 136–146.

Lesley, M. (2008). Access and resistance to dominant forms of discourse: Critical literacy and "at risk" high school students. *Literacy Research & Instruction. 47,* 174–194.

———. (2009). "You gotta read it with awake in you": Marginalized high school readers, engagement, and reading as performance. In J. Richards and C. Lassonde (Eds.), *Evidence-based quality literacy tutoring programs: What works and why.* (pp. 46–55). Newark, DE: International Reading Association.

Lewis, M. (1993). *Without a word: Teaching beyond women's silence.* New York: Routledge.

Luke, C., & Gore, J. (1992). *Feminisms and critical pedagogy.* New York: Routledge.

Mahiri, J. (2004). *What they don't learn in school: Literacy in the lives of urban youth.* New York, NY: Peter Lang Publishers.

Moje, E. (2000). "To be part of the story": The literacy practices of gangsta adolescents. *Teachers College Record, 102* (3), 651–690.

Moje, E., McIntosh, A., Ciechanowski, K., Kramer, K., Ellis, L., Carrillo, R., & Collazo, T. (2004). Working toward third space in content area literacy: An examination of everyday funds of knowledge and discourse. *Reading Research Quarterly, 39* (1), 38–70.

Moje, E., Overby, M., Tysvaer, N., & Morris, K. (2008). The complex world of adolescent literacy: Myths, motivations, and mysteries. *Harvard Educational Review, 78* (1), 107–154.

Moore, D., & Cunningham J. (2006). Adolescent agency and literacy. In D. Alvermann, K. Hinchman, D. Moore, S. Phelps, and D. Waff (Eds.), *Reconceptualizing the literacies in adolescents' lives.* (pp. 129–146). Mahwah, NJ; Lawrence Erlbaum and Associates.

National Council of Teachers of English. (2006, April). *NCTE principles of adolescent literacy reform.* Urbana, IL: Author. Retrieved October 5, 2006, from http://ncte.org.

National Council of Teachers of English. (2007). *NCTE policy research brief on adolescent literacy.* Urbana, IL: Author. Retrieved October 5, 2009, from http://www.org/library/NCTEFiles/Resources/PolicyResearchAdolLitResearchBrief.pdf.

Pipher, M. (1994). *Reviving Ophelia: Saving the selves of adolescent girls.* New York: Ballentine.

Reed, J., Schallert, D., Beth, A., & Woodruff, A. (2004). Motivated reader, engaged writer: The role of motivation in the literate acts of adolescents. In T. Jetton and J. Dole (Eds.), *Adolescent literacy research and practice.* (pp. 251–282). New York: The Guilford Press.

Reynolds, M. (2004). *I won't read and you can't make me: Reaching reluctant teen readers.* Portsmouth, NH: Heinemann.

Rycik, J., & Irvin, J. (2001). *What adolescents deserve: A commitment to students' literacy learning.* Newark, DE, International Reading Association.

Skeggs, B. (2008). The problem with identity. In A. Yin (Ed.), *Problematizing identity: Everyday struggles in language, culture, and education. (pp. 11–34).* New York: Lawrence Erlbaum Associates.

Williams, B. (2006). Metamorphosis hurts: Resistant students and myths of transformation. *Journal of Adolescent & Adult Literacy, 50* (2), 148–153.

Chapter Two

"I Got No Place Else to Go after School": Theories and Narratives of What Places Adolescent Girls "At Risk" for Dropping Out of School

Narrative Profile of Isabel

In sixth grade, Isabel, a small Latina girl with a sprinkling of freckles and dark flashing eyes, joined the writing group without any outward trepidation of being with girls who were seventh and eighth graders and who had been together in the group the previous year. Although she was petite, Isabel had a way of lifting her chin and insisting on respect with a narrowed, "I'm not afraid of you" glint. In the writing group, Isabel was by turns guarded and candid, sensitive and tough, friendly and sullen.

In sixth and seventh grade Isabel described her family life in brief clips with few details. For two years, I knew little more about Isabel's relationship with her mom other than she left when Isabel was too little to remember, reappeared in Isabel's life when she was eight, then disappeared again until Isabel turned thirteen. The first time Isabel's mother returned to her life, Isabel said she mostly remembered being afraid she was going to be taken away from her father and stepmother. Although Isabel had no knowledge of where her mother lived in the intervening years of her absences, Isabel's dad did not want her real mom to be a "stranger" to Isabel and accordingly allowed for such sporadic contact. At age thirteen Isabel described her relationship with her mother from the point of view of her father's logic of not wanting her mother to be a stranger to her and yet such limited contact did little to familiarize Isabel with her mother. In sixth and seventh grade Isabel often wrote idealistic odes about her mother such as the following:

My mom is real sweet
She makes me feel protected
She makes me feel good

In eighth grade, Isabel's mother made a concerted effort to re-connect with her by picking Isabel up from school every day. In spite of these efforts, Isabel spoke at length about her extreme conflict over her relationship with her mother. On one hand, Isabel wanted to be close with her mother. On the other hand, Isabel was deeply angry at her mother for abandoning her and stated she could never forgive her mother for leaving. She could not escape the loss she felt on Mother's Day, the humiliation of having to shop for clothes in "girls' stores" with her father, or the trauma of being investigated by Child Protective Services because a teacher thought she lived in a household without a mother and deemed this to be an unsuitable situation for an adolescent girl.

One of the few details Isabel volunteered about her father had to do with her father's anger. Isabel stated her father would yell at her, chase her, and threaten her until she cowered and cried when he was angry. She explained nonchalantly while composing an essay about her father's anger, "When I cry in front of my dad when my dad yells at me and I start crying, right, he'll say 'I'm sorry.'"

During the years Isabel participated in the writing group, she struggled to maintain a friendship with two other girls in the group. When they were in sixth grade, the three girls formed a clique. By the middle of their seventh grade year, the two other girls decided to drop Isabel as a friend. The other girls explained their friendship issues were due to the fact that Isabel often lied and was unpredictably angry. I learned of the rift in a quiet and matter-of-fact, "we're not friends anymore" statement at the beginning of one of the writing group sessions a few minutes before Isabel's arrival. After this event, the three girls did not resume a friendship for the remainder of their seventh and eighth grade years.

One day the school's principal happened to come into the library just as our writing group was beginning. Isabel hopped up from her computer where she was slowly preparing to retype another poem about her mother she held clutched in her hand on an inky piece of notebook paper. "Look what I wrote!" she called to the principal as she bounded into his path. I remember thinking Isabel's energy reminded me of a small child jumping up and down in front of a parent, demanding attention. The principal stopped long enough to read the poem and tell Isabel he liked it. When the principal left, Isabel sluggishly returned to her slow retyping of the poem on the computer but picked up more interest in writing after she informed me she was going to give the poem to her stepmother, a new audience to compose the poem for.

In her interview at the end of the project, Isabel nervously pushed the sleeves of her sweatshirt up to reveal several rings of dark purple bruises.

When she saw me looking at her arm, she quickly lowered her sleeves and stated, "My stepmom worries about me when I get bruises and stuff like this one." Isabel explained she had bruised her arm through playing on a trampoline with her cousin and waking suddenly from a nap and bumping into something then added, "But my dad wants me to cover it up, so no one will think wrong."

At the end of two years of participation in the writing project, Isabel described herself as an "ok" writer and added, "I just don't like to write unless I feel mad or bored." The one goal she stated for her writing ability was she wished she could improve in her use of vocabulary—learn to use "bigger words" that would make her sound more intelligent. At the end of the third year, Isabel reiterated that she had "to be in the mood" to write and stated her goals for writing were to write a book "about feelings, expressions, and meanings about how life should be like in the real world because life isn't just a fairytale." Isabel explained further, "When you go to sleep, you can think it's a fairytale, but when you wake up it has to be reality." Isabel always wrote about her reality with friends, school, boys, and her mother. During the second year she participated in the group, Isabel wrote the following piece about friendship.

Friends turning their back

At the fist of the year I and some people were friends but as the year went on we started separating. Me and one of my friends started getting mad and stop talking because she started treating an another girl better than me. We look at each other just look at her But we don't talk anymore she'll say hi but I'll ignore her. I guess she thinks she is better than me but I told her that we are all a like that she is no different than me. Her and that girl have been friends since last year and me and her have been friends since the 2nd grade so then you have a problem

For Isabel forming trusting relationships was important yet difficult. This piece of Isabel's writing also captured a key element of trust and agency in peer friendships that all of the girls wrote about or discussed in the writing group sessions. As such, this sample of Isabel's writing exemplified the ways the girls in the writing group were simultaneously vulnerable and resistant to the actions and opinions of peers who served to undermine their experiences in school. In fact, peers played a pivotal role in the girls' discernment of trusting relationships, gender roles, and Discourse communities.

In order to complicate the dialogue surrounding programs and research agendas concerned with at-risk populations of learners, in this chapter I consider the ways the term "at-risk" has been used to describe adolescents like Isabel by various educational entities. I also compare such descriptions to the writings and discussions of the girls in the writing group, all of whom had been previously identified as at risk for dropping out of high school due to their aptitude in school and/or family circumstances. Finally, I address the ways the girls were distracted from academic achievement by the social milieu they participated in including peer relationships, gender roles, and a social detachment from school forms of Discourse.

Competing Theories of "At-Risk" and "Struggling" Adolescents

As I was writing this chapter, I received the following e-mail from a first-year teacher on the brink of resignation:

Dear Dr. Lesley,

I am nearing the end of my first semester as a seventh grade writing teacher, and, although I see some progress being made, I feel helpless. I realize many first year teachers go through various metamorphoses, but I don't want to use that as a crutch. I honestly feel the same way Erin Gruwell felt as a first year teacher, "this isn't how I had it pictured." Every day I send students to the office for fighting, cursing me and/or their classmates, sticking their chests in my face as if they want to fight, or slamming books on the floor or their desks if I reprimand them; two weeks ago, I was shot in the eye with pencil lead.

In my community, for the majority of my students, education is just not a priority at home; it never will be. Many come from illiterate parents, abusive homes, and a long line of drug usage. Realistically I know I am not a miracle worker (as cliché as that sounds), but I want to teach these kids.

In the midst of the words describing her classroom and community, this first-year teacher was grappling with both a stereotypic perspective (Franklin, 2000) of her students' home environments as one placing them at risk for learning and a sincere desire to teach her students to write successfully for academic purposes. This teacher's struggle to engage at-risk students in writing methods touted as "best practice" in her teacher preparation program is a concern I have heard echoed by numerous educators. Whether it is due to the teaching methods, perceived home environment of students, or school culture, teachers themselves often struggle with teaching "struggling" learners.

In recent decades, a great deal has been written about at-risk students in the field of education. Much of this work has given rise to outreach and intervention initiatives at the local, state, and federal level (e.g., 21st Century Grants, Communities in Schools, Reading First). Discursive practices and definitions surrounding the moniker "at-risk" have also been met with criticism for containing discriminatory ideologies implied through student subjectivities derived from deficit, "disease" model labels of student ability. The extent to which labels such as "at-risk" and "struggling" (an often synonymous term used in literacy studies) describe social constructions and normative theories of student success and failure lies at the heart of this debate.

The words "at risk" when applied to learners are used in general to refer to students who are failing or nearly failing in school for reasons of cognitive, behavioral, economic, political, socio-cultural, or combinations of these phenomena (Bailey, 2006). The label "at-risk" has been used virtually interchangeably with terms such as "struggling," "disenfranchised," "marginalized," "striving," "inexperienced," and even "urban" (see Dutro & Zenkov, 2008). While researchers have made important distinctions between these terms with respect to social constructions of identity, the impetus behind such labels is largely one of discerning reasons for why some students are successful in school and others are not (Triplett, 2007).

In the field of literacy education, a great deal of research pertaining to at-risk adolescents involves research on "struggling" adolescent readers. Concerns surrounding struggling adolescent readers and writers have been gaining increased attention in current federal policy statements, funding, and professional development initiatives (Alliance for Excellent Education, 2006). As such, the field of literacy is awash in dialogues pertaining to struggling adolescent readers and writers (Beers, 2003; Beers, Probst, & Rief, 2007). A past president of the International Reading Association insisted on such a mandate, identifying research pertaining to struggling adolescent readers as an area deserving much more attention (Vogt, 2004/2005). Since this declaration was made, awareness of the need for research focused on the literacy acquisition of struggling adolescent readers and writers has reached a critical juncture. At the heart of the matter lie differences in the definitions of what constitutes a struggling learner. Triplett (2007) found definitions of struggling readers to be fundamentally social constructions. Alvermann (2001) delineated four theoretical models of reasons why adolescents struggle with literacy as the following: (1) cultural mismatch theories, (2) deprivation theories, (3) difference theories, and (4) normative theories.

In Alvermann's synthesis of the body of research on struggling adolescent readers, cultural mismatch theories define struggling learners as students who do not have previous experiences with school expectations for literacy including linguistic and metalinguistic experiences. These students are deemed to be behind their counterparts who come from backgrounds that mirror school definitions, values, and expectations for literacy. As these students get older, they are often identified as struggling readers through their attitudes towards school reading tasks. Many cease to participate in school literacy curricula. Deprivation theories of struggling readers entail students who do not perform well on literacy tasks as measured by standardized, performance-based, or informal assessments and teacher observations. These are students who are deemed to possess cognitive processing problems that interfere with their ability to learn successfully in school settings. Difference theories of struggling adolescent readers include students who have the potential to perform at grade level with learning tasks but do not because of the type of instruction they receive. These students may be deemed to struggle with learning because of developmentally inappropriate instruction or because of culturally unresponsive instruction. The bottom line is that in this theory students need different instruction in order to be successful. Finally, normative theories of struggling adolescent readers posit that students are idiosyncratically placed into the position of being a struggling reader based on a larger social need to label students' academic ability relative to an arbitrarily determined norm. In effect, someone has to struggle in order to identify "successful" readers. As Franzak (2006) summarized, "the definition of reading achievement necessitates the identity of failure" (p. 231). Each of the theoretical models Alvermann identified teeter on a wedge of blame and implied responsibility. In doing so, these models provide compelling evidence for the necessity of student and teacher agency.

Much like critiques of the term "struggling," "at-risk" as a label has been denounced for contributing to images of feckless children and adolescents lacking in any sense of self-control or agency. Often missing from discussions of the label "at-risk" is the resilience of students contending with social settings and school policies that serve to inhibit their learning (Franklin, 2000; Franzak, 2006). As such, explanations of the term "at-risk" have been critiqued for being awkwardly perched on discriminatory ideals. For example, Franklin (2000) argued against using the term "at-risk" so as not to foster a "disease model" vision of poor, minority youth. Franklin wrote,

> Unfortunately, use of the risk paradigm in the educational setting has engendered more victim blaming and labeling as it relates to poor and minority children. In its attempt to help remediate and provide equal education for poor and minority students by identifying those who may be at risk for academic failure, it has systematically indicted many students with its "disease-model" concentration. (p. 5)

Some research concerned with "at-risk" learners has fueled such negative images through studies predicated upon a deficit model of learning and a view of a student's at-risk status being monolithic in nature (Dutro &

Zenkov, 2008). Even though scholars have problematized notions of being marginalized or silenced in sometimes esoteric discussions of what it means to be placed or place oneself on the margins of schooling (e.g., Moje, 2000), most research focused on at-risk students is largely concerned with addressing the situation or "ecological framework" that led to such a label (Franklin, 2000). A great deal of this research has been devoted to intervention programs targeting parental involvement, early reading, after-school programs, and community-based programs (Bailey, 2006; Richman, Rosenfeld, & Bowen, 1998). In fact, many educational entities are deeply concerned with meeting the needs of students deemed to be at risk for academic failure. Federal funding for at-risk students through 21st Century Grants, Striving Reader's Grants and Reading First Grants are examples of federal initiatives that have been created in response to this concern.

Tensions Inherent in the Term "At-Risk"

Years ago I brought several high school students who were identified as at risk to speak to a class of pre-service teachers seeking secondary-level certification. The high school coordinator from the students' school introduced them as "at-risk" students to the pre-service teachers. At the conclusion of the discussion, one of the high school students asked me what "at-risk" meant. I responded, "It means being at-risk for dropping out of high school." The student looked slapped by my frank and simplified statement and replied indignantly, "That's an insult. I'm not going to drop out of high school!" This experience lingered in my conciousness and led me to wonder about the extent to which the girls participating in the writing group viewed themselves as being academically at risk.

Educators and researchers balk at the label "at-risk" and yet turn to it as a way to describe a particular educational phenomenon. This tension comes from two competing notions surrounding use of the term "at-risk":

1. using the term "at-risk" to serve as a rationale for intervention programs designed to support marginalized students, and
2. questioning the discursive practices and definitions associated with use of the term "at-risk" for fear that such discussions may in actuality serve to alienate students from school settings.

Some educators see the number of students falling through the educational cracks of accountability, struggling with social alienation, and ultimately dropping out of school. NAEP data, graduation and attrition rates, and college readiness studies (Wise, 2009) point to the fact that public education is failing large demographic swaths of students in the United States. This data has prompted the creation of new accountability measures such as college readiness standards and the rise of intervention programs for students deemed to be at risk for dropping out of high school. Such concern also captures the perspective of the federally funded program through which I encountered the girls who participated in this study.[1]

The other view of the term "at-risk" is a critique of the deficit message inherent in this label. Research formulated from this perspective falls into Alvermann's cultural mismatch and normative models due to the "funds of knowledge" and resources at-risk students possess that are often overlooked in school settings (Dutro & Zenkov, 2008; Moll et al., 1992). Similar critiques of the deficit tenor of at-risk labels have suggested adopting a broadened, multiple literacies view of at-risk adolescents in order to illustrate "that these adolescents are capable and literate if we view them from the perspective of multiliteracies in new times" (O'Brien, 2001).

Making a similar argument about deficit models of learners, Delpit (1995) critiqued dialogues surrounding best practices in writing instruction for excluding the views of African American educators. Of this omitted perspective Delpit wrote:

> It is time to look closely at elements of our educational system, particularly those elements we consider progressive; time to see whether there is minority involvement and support, and if not, to ask why; time to reassess what we are doing in public schools and universities to include other voices, other experiences; time to seek the diversity in our educational movements that we talk about seeking in our class-rooms. (p. 20)

This "silenced dialogue" Delpit noted is reminiscent of the discussion surrounding definitions of at-risk students in that more dialogue is needed that draws meaning from the individuals considered to be at risk. Similarly Franklin (2000) posited,

> Research studies on risk and resilience must incorporate the subjective experiences of poor and minority youth. . . . If a young person does not perceive elements in their environment to be traumatic and achievement limiting, then a researcher's notion of "at risk" or "resilient" may be ignoring key attributional information. (p. 10)

To label adolescents as "at-risk" may serve to undermine the resourcefulness and available social support networks often made invisible by such labels. To

---

[1] Please see the Communities in Schools website at cisnet.org for more information about their mission.

ignore factors that threaten adolescents' academic success may also serve to compromise their academic potential. Consequently, I think the solution to the critique in favor of and in opposition to identifying students as at risk is to address both concerns while considering the unique subjectivities of individual students.

Secondary Scenes and Social Phenomena That Place Adolescent Girls At Risk

Three conditions emerged in this project as the primary obstacles that served to undermine the girls' participation in the Third Space writing group. These conditions consisted of mistrust in peer friendships, gender identities tied to restrictive dating roles, and intellectual distancing from school forms of Discourse and literacy. The girls' narratives on these topics shed light on issues the girls felt confused or burdened by. Notably, behavioral expectations in each of these narrative themes were greatly shaped by peers.

The girls made references consistently about the ways peers affected their use of digital literacies, Discourses, and attitudes about boys and gender roles much more so than parents or teachers. In fact, it was not uncommon for the girls to keep their *MySpace* accounts, text messages, and dating experiences entirely secret from their parents. Furthermore, the girls spoke of the deleterious effects of untrustworthy friendships, male dating aggression, and text messaging jargon, yet they put up with such experiences in order to be part of various peer-driven social groups and Discourse communities. Parents and other significant adults in the girls' lives often tried to provide social support and critique about friends, dating, and digital literacies; however, these messages were rarely mentioned in the girls' narratives depicting the day-to-day interactions of peer cultures that often placed them in hostile and subordinate roles.

Trust and Fragile Allegiances

One February afternoon, I became aware of a rift in Isabel's clique of three Latina, seventh grade girls.

ML: Where is Isabel? Have you seen Isabel?

Felicia: We're not friends anymore.

ML: You're not friends with *Isabel*?

Felicia: She got an attitude with us on the bus and started yelling at us.

Kiara: No. She started yelling at us, "Get away from me!" and I wanted to tell her something.

HK[My GA]: Do you live close to each other or do you ride the same bus [to go to school]?

Felicia: No. We were on the bus uh for CS [competitive sports].

Kiara: She said, "Get away from me and take your smart mouths with you." "I'm sick of all of you!" And, I said, "You got a smart mouth, and I'm sick of you too!" She said, "I don't care," and I said "Shut up." And, what else did you say [speaking to Felicia] What else did she say? Uh [inaudible] "Whatever." And, so I went to sit in the front of the bus. And, we're done!

HK: [Referring to the candy I brought for the girls.] Do any of y'all like special dark [chocolate]?

Kiara: I do!

Felicia: I don't know.

HK: Oops sorry.

Isabel: [Arriving to the group.] Can I have one?

Felicia: No.

Kiara: There ain't no more. Them girls jacked the bag! [Referring to a group of 8th grade girls in the group.]

On the surface, this exchange entailed an account of a secondary scene from the writing group in which middle school girls argued with one another in an instantaneous volley of angry and parroted words. *"I'm sick of all of you!/I'm sick of you too!"* Beneath the surface of these words, however, lay a fragile allegiance where vulnerability and mistrust were made visible through references to an untrustworthy "smart mouth" who should "shut up." Essentially, the fight started when Isabel would not let her friends know why she was upset and pushed them away abruptly and unexpectedly. Felicia and Kiara responded by mirroring Isabel's anger, turned against her with a decision not to be her "friend" any longer, and days later placed her on the margins of the writing group through tepid shrugs to Isabel's attempts to communicate with them and by lying about the chocolate candy I had brought for the girls.

    Later on in the same writing session, sitting physically ostracized from the group at a separate bank of computers, Isabel confided to me that she became upset on the bus because her dad had become livid with her coach after the basketball game but proceeded to take out his anger on her instead of the coach. Isabel reacted to her father's obscenities and threats by turning on her friends and destroying their trust in her for the last time. Isabel then isolated herself on the back of the bus, riding alone in the dark with a rush of angry words in her head. A few days later, Isabel wrote her account of the incident in the writing group.

THE DAY I GOT MAD!!!!!

It was write after are game my dad called me and told me that he was going to come and pick me up at [another middle school] so I told my coach and she said for me to call my dad and tell him that he had to go to [her middle school] to pick me up. My dad got mad and started yelling at me so when I got on the bus I started crying and when felicia, Kiara and Anna came to see what was wrong I yelled at them and told them to go away but then they started talking about me so I said "for them to shut up cause I don't need there smart mouth right now"!!!!! The coach told them to go to the front because they didn't want them to be around me right now. Well when we got to the school my dad was waiting out side in the parking lot, waiting to chew me out in front of everyone. When I got off the bus he stared telling me, "You need to fu**ing get your sh** straight girl cause if you don't than im going to take your little a** out of ca and tell them fu**ing coaches off an then throw the fu**ing finger at them when were leaving out the door." When I got home I told my mom and my mom started yelling at my dad so to get my mom to shut up he had to say his sorry so he went in and told me to get a schedule from my coaches and he said he was sorry for yelling at me because he went to far this time.

A little later in the same writing group session, I tried to coax Felicia and Kiara into talking with Isabel.

ML: So are you still mad at Isabel?

Kiara: Yeah.

ML: You know what, she was having a rough time with her dad. I don't think she was being rude to you just—

Felicia: But she always lies about that stuff, I'm not lying.

Kiara: Yeah she has to make up stuff. She makes up all kinds of stuff just to make us to like feel bad for her.

Felicia: 'Cuz she tells us something and then the next day she is telling everybody something else.

Kiara: She was telling us, that, okay, this person that was talking to her and she got R-A-P-E-D.

ML: Really? When did this happen?

Kiara: A long time ago and she tells us and every time she tells us she tells us something different. "Like I didn't tell you it was in the alley, I said it was in the house!" And then the next time, "I didn't say *that*" she always changes everything.

ML: So you don't really believe it ever happened?

Kiara: Yeah, I don't. And "my cousin we were in the alley throwing trash" and then the next time "we were in the bedroom and my dad had a friend over" and she keeps changing. So I don't believe her.

ML: So what do you think? Do you think she has been victimized or do you think it's never happened. Or, do you think it's happened more than once?

Kiara: I don't think it's happened.

ML: You don't think it's happened more than once?

Kiara: No. At the same time she was in the house and the other time she was in the alley—somewhere I don't know. She told me two different places but had every-thing the same.

ML: So you think she says that just for attention?

Kiara: Yeah.

Felicia: There's a lot of girls do that.

Kiara: Like Felicia.

Felicia: I don't do that.

Kiara: I know. Your stories are true, and I could find out if you are lying or not. Cuz I don't like people to lie to me.

Through this exchange, Kiara and Felicia explained their expectations for honesty in friendships. Violating their code of honesty resulted in Isabel being ignored by Kiara and Felicia in the writing group for the remainder of their seventh grade year. In establishing their code, Kiara and Felicia also positioned themselves in opposition to Isabel and other girls who lie about being raped. The undertones of this exchange pointed to a larger dichotomy of adolescent girls formed around a polarity of girls who lie and girls who do not lie.

I included these excerpts in this chapter addressing at-risk learners be-cause these passages demonstrate the fundamental element of trust in all of the girls' lives that emerged as a central component of their behavior in the group. Trust and the lack thereof was something the girls spoke of frequently and wrote about in narratives of peer friendships. Trust tied to truth was of particular importance. Namely, as these excerpts demonstrate the girls grappled with whether or not they could trust their friends with the truth of their life experiences and whether they could trust their friends to tell the truth.

The narratives in the above exchanges also presented victimization themes where being a victim was scrutinized through the lens of trust. Lying as a way to cope with victimization was another narrative theme that cropped up in Isabel's confession to me about why she was mean to her friends as well as in Kiara's lying to Isabel about the chocolates being stolen by other girls in the group. Such lies were justified in the girls' narratives as a way to redress feeling wronged.

Clustered together with trust issues, spreading gossip and keeping secrets were often mentioned in narratives involving friends and trust. Similarly, teasing and its attendant social ostracization were also key to forming trusting friendships. For example, in another clique of African American girls, Alicia was often targeted for public ridicule by Tara. One afternoon in the writing group when Alicia and Tara were in seventh grade, Alicha sat off to the side of the group with her coat zipped up stifling tears and wrote:

> *It all happened today in writing club when Tara said by the time Alicia gets done pouring the chips they are going to be all gone and when she said that I felt so sad because I think she ment I was fat and that just went to me and so I just stared crying and then I put my mean face on and she said I can look like that two and I said what then she said don't get mad because you can't sit over here and I said I am not mad because I don't want to sit over there.*

Alicia's narrative demonstrated the subtleties of teasing and maintaining trusting relationships with peers. Furthermore, Alicia was extremely vulnerable to the negative comments and perceptions of her friend Tara. Tara's words had a great deal of power over Alicia's perception of the social milieu involved in membership of the writing group (e.g., ostracizing Alicia from the group) as well as membership in a Discourse community where a reference to distribution of snacks was tantamount to calling her "fat." Both acts socially alienated Alicia without warning. Such Discourse, much like Isabel's eruption of anger on the bus, was a violation of trust in the fragile terrain of adolescent girls fending for themselves in social contexts where adult messages are unavailable or out of synch with the coping strategies the girls resorted to.

Gendered Views of Themselves

In tandem to the ways peer relationships undermined the girls' level of participation in the writing group, gendered views of dating roles served to monopolize much of the girls' focus surrounding writing. Dating boys was another prevalent theme in the girls' narratives. These narratives revealed all of the girls were preoccupied with creating or maintaining a dating relationship with boys. Further, the depictions of these relationships often offered the girls limited roles to occupy in a dating relationship and as such were stereotypic in nature. In my analysis of the girls' writing I discovered the following beliefs or Discourse models (Gee, 2005) of gender and dating roles the girls held:

1. Marriage and having a boyfriend is a status symbol, a goal practiced through imagined relationships with pretend celebrity husbands and boyfriends.
2. Ideal boys to date are physically attractive and older.
3. The number of "cute" boys listed as "friends" on a girl's *MySpace* account is a status symbol.
4. A girl's power in a dating relationship is defined by her physical attractiveness to boys.
5. Stealing another girl's boyfriend is acceptable if the girl is not deemed to meet physical and behavioral standards for being desirable to boys.
6. It is inevitable that boys will break a girl's heart; dating and heartache are an ominous and unavoidable prospect.
7. Girls should take blame for boys' behavior towards them.
8. Girls face implicit rewards and consequences for meeting or not meeting peers' expectations for ideal female characteristics and dating roles.

Needless to say, the media and popular culture texts played a significant role in reinforcing and shaping girls' understandings of dating behaviors.

In addition to the writing the girls did during the writing group about dating, the girls routinely posted messages on their *MySpace* accounts that revealed highly sexualized expectations for gender roles in dating relationships. For example, in the summer between her seventh and eighth grade years, Veronica downloaded the following statement from "My Hot Comments" and posted it to her *MySpace* page, "You've been a naughty boy! Now go to my room." Messages such as this one dripping with sexual innuendo were prevalent in the girls' *MySpace* sites. These messages depicting an emboldened and even reckless persona belied the cautious approach to designing *MySpace* pages described by the girls. Attention to anticipated male audiences led the girls to write messages specifically focused on not offending their current or potential boyfriends. Veronica spoke at length about the role her boyfriend played in designing her *MySpace* page in terms of the way she encoded messages to him in her "status" (e.g., single, in a relationship, etc.) and "mood" updates. As such, Veronica's posting "You've been a naughty boy! Now go to my room" may have been indicative of her playing out a socially prescribed dating role of appearing to be sexually available in order to allure her boyfriend more so than taking on a sexually aggressive persona in a dating relationship.

Beyond such blurbs and images from the girls' *MySpace* pages, writing about dating within the group manifested in three genres of writing: (1) fictional stories of being married to or dating celebrities (e.g., Chris Brown), (2) personal narratives about dating experiences, and (3) love poetry written to boys in both real and imagined relationships. Within these genres of writing the girls were by turns carnivalesque and fatalistic in their descriptions of dating. For example, in the latter half of her eighth grade year, Adrianna wrote the following poem:

Love

There a time were you fall for the
one you love you reach into his
arms the day you start to cry. He
leans into your ear and say the
four letter word I love you girl to
the day that my life goes bye, you
say hes your baby the times go
through times get thick sometimes
thin but he is still your boo you
still sit back and think why he is
the one for me.

In this poem, Adrianna constructed a persona of herself as someone who is reflecting on a long-term relationship that has endured many hardships. In doing so, she presented a view of "true love" as a relationship that survives trials through time and continues to evoke an undying commitment and emotional bond. This writing stands in stark contrast to the message on Veronica's *MySpace* page, yet both samples are indicative of the extent to which being someone's girlfriend was a highly prized social role. These examples also demonstrate the stereotypic dichotomy between the demure, loyal girl in Adrianna's poem and the domineering, sexually aggressive girl in Veronica's copied message—two ends of a spectrum depicting dating roles for girls both containing victimization undertones.

Adrianna, who was one of the most prolific writers in the group, stopped attending the writing group when it met after school because one of her friends wanted to spend this time flirting with boys posed on the sidewalks and walls surrounding the entrance to the school. On several occasions, Adrianna came to the group and then left a few minutes after her friend arrived at the door whispering in her ear and tugging on her arm to go. After a few weeks of her friend's insistence on pursuing boys, Adrianna finally quit coming to the group altogether.

At Risk as Writers in School Settings

In individual interviews, all of the girls talked about the extent to which social forms of literacy and peer Discourse communities dictated their literacy development. While the girls felt almost forced to use text messaging jargon in the notes written for peers and postings on their *MySpace* pages in order to participate in peer groups, they simultaneously articulated a distanced view of school expectations for writing. Namely, school forms of writing were absent from their discussions about personal reasons for writing. In the Third Space setting where I worked with the girls, such references to school writing rarely emerged in the midst of their composing processes. One example occurred at the beginning of the second year of the project. In this first writing group session of the final year, I started by asking the girls to establish goals for our group. The following is an excerpt from this discussion.

ML: So, it might just be better for us to go right to the library and have snacks that we can have around the computer and then do some writing. Is everybody up for that? . . . What else do you want to do this semester?

Tara: Um, I don't know.

ML: Do you want to publish some more? More often than once a year? The last two years we've done one little publication.

Isabel: Can we publish like one every two or three months?

Tara: Yeah I'm down.

ML: Let's try to publish more frequently. [Inaudible] So, what would you think about having a wall somewhere where we put our writing up where people could walk by and read it? Would you like that? Yes or no?

Tara: Not with our names on it.

ML: Were you all embarrassed when people read these [referring to last year's book the girls created of their writing] around the school?

Isabel: No, I was showing everybody.

ML: Were you proud? I mean some of the stuff you wrote was very personal. Is that okay?

Tara: [In a joking tone.] Nothing, nothing's personal because I tell everybody everything.

ML: These are really good. All of your writing. So good. I'm so proud of all of you. Okay anything else you want to do? What about some of your goals for writing? Is there anything you want to learn how to do as a writer?

Felicia: Make our stories interesting.

Tara: Yeah.

ML: How to make your stories interesting?

Tara: I want to learn . . . um . . . what are they called? Question marks . . . not question marks.

ML: Punctuation?

Tara: Yeah in the right places. Because I always keep putting them in the wrong places.

In this exchange two goals for writing are suggested that carry a tone reminiscent of school expectations for "good" writing: (1) ways to make writing more interesting and (2) how to use punctuation correctly. The first request for instruction connotes an understanding of the rhetorical role a sense of audience plays in crafting writing. The second request connotes an understanding of accuracy in using punctuation more than likely derived from school experiences. In noting these goals, the girls demonstrated fairly sophisticated notions of writing and yet indicated a barrier to such aspects of writing. They mimicked teacher talk about style and conventions of writing and yet did not similarly offer strategies for developing skills in these areas as writers. Even so, this exchange demonstrated a willingness and desire to learn school criteria for writing on the part of the girls in a setting where they felt safe to ask for this help.

This exchange and other similar references to standardized writing tests highlighted the fact that the girls received the message they were lacking in writing skills, but they did not also receive a sense of ways to overcome these shortfalls in their writing ability through their previous instruction. To counteract this gap in understanding, they turned to peers and themselves to acquire a sense of control and acceptance as writers using media such as *MySpace*, text messaging, handwritten notes to friends, and private words scrawled into journals at home. These nonschool forms of writing provided spaces where new punctuation rules and new criteria for what makes writing interesting could be applied without judgment on the quality of the writing in terms of style and convention. The scrutiny this kind of writing faced was based fundamentally on the social messages inscribed in the writing (e.g., messages that disrespect or elevate friends and boyfriends).

Towards the end of her eighth grade year, Veronica wrote the following blog on her *MySpace* account.

> WaT Up WiTh ThE WoRld. LyFe iS TiReRiNg WiTh aL DiS hAtE FrM PpL sTaRtiNg StUfF, PpL r hUqTiN, ChIlDrEn R cRyN, BuT YeT We cOnTiNuE oN. Do U eVa tHiNg bOuT Da PpL uR aFfEdTiNg ArOuNd U. NOPE. u JuSt WoRrieD BoUt LoOkn gOoD 4 Ur HoMiEs. U TrYn To OuR LiVe ThE pAiN u FeEl whEn iT aImt gOiNg NoWhErE. SO STOP PrEtEnDiNg To Be WhO eVeRyOnE WnTs U to Be. JUST BE U. *TIME FOR ME TO BE ME ALREADY*

Veronica's writing on her *MySpace* blog demonstrated the division between conventions of print in an adolescent Discourse community situated on *MySpace* and the reference to "interesting" writing and punctuation expectations outlined for adolescents in school settings. I do not know who Veronica had in mind as an audience when she composed this blog, but I am fairly certain she did not intend this writing to be turned in for a school assignment.

Implications for Literacy Instruction with At-Risk Adolescent Girls

Similar to previous studies that describe at-risk students as feeling "alienated" (Hamovich, 1997, p. 2) from school, the girls in the writing group reported a lack of relevancy for school literacy instruction. The same social elements that competed with the girls for fully engaging in the Third Space writing group were also present in regular classroom settings. To minimize social issues that serve to undermine adolescent girls' participation in classroom literacy learning and place them at risk for school failure, I recommend the following based on my work with these girls.

First, adolescent girls need to feel a level of trust with peers and teachers in order to develop as writers. They need to feel safe to make mistakes and learn how to address mistakes. In this vein, adolescent girls such as the ones in this study benefit from extended experiences with writing that are not challenged by an uncomfortable audience. As such, peer review and writer's workshop formats for writing instruction should be staved off until such time that the students feel enough confidence in their writing to withstand external judgment. Also, such work with peers should proceed after students have developed a trusting relationship with the teacher as well.

Second, adolescent girls need curriculum that will empower them to construct less gender-limiting identities centered on stereotypic dating roles. While I made an attempt at this with activities such as analyzing the images and roles of adolescent girls in the media and reading Flake's book (2004) *Who Am I Without Him?* I learned the girls needed to engage in analysis of their primary, lived experiences with boys much more so than examining secondary sources on this topic. Autobiographical and narrative writing became a key resource for such an endeavor.

Third, literacy instruction needs to include writing in different social registers such as text messaging jargon. The complexity of such nonschool forms of writing needs to be validated for students and offered as a bridge into mastering academic modes of writing. The girls in this study had sophisticated rules for writing in nonschool venues. Such mastery of the rules governing various adolescent Discourse communities indicate an aptitude with writing that could be translated into reasons for adhering to more traditional academic rules for writing in school settings. An understanding of mores, codes, and expectations for writing in one context can lead to an understanding of expectations for writing in another context.

Concluding Vignette: "Because I Got No Place Else to Go After School"

Halfway through my second year into this project, Tia sat frozen with a stoic expression on her face as she held a pencil in her hand and not making any effort to generate a list of potential topics she could write about. When I asked Tia why she was not writing, she stated, "I don't like writing because it's too much work. It's easier to say it instead of taking the time to write it all out." Attempting a playful tone, I asked Tia why she attended the writing group if she hated to write. Without hesitation or change in her dulled demeanor, Tia responded, "Because I got no place else to go after school." This statement stilled my jovial affect as I considered the depth of her words. Indeed for many adolescent girls there is no place for them to go after school in the immediate sense of a school day as well as the longer-term sense of a stalled education beyond a K-12 setting. Although Tia may not have had the latter in mind about her attendance in the writing group, her words spoke to the dim view of academic writing and the dead-end statistic too many low socio-economic status, ethnically diverse adolescent girls experience in school settings.

References

Alliance for Excellent Education, (2004, December). Adolescent literacy [Fact sheet]. Washington, DC: Author. Retrieved September 20, 2005, from http://www.all4ed.ort/publications/Reading Next/AdolescentLiteracyFactSheet

Alvermann, D. (2001). Reading adolescents' reading identities: Looking back to see ahead. *Journal of Adolescent & Adult Literacy, 44* (8), 676–690.

Bailey, L. (2006). Examining gifted students who are economically at-risk to determine factors that influence their early reading success. *Early Childhood Education Journal, 33* (5), 307–315.

Beers, K. (2003). *When kids can't read: What teachers can do.* Portsmouth, NH: Heinemann.

Beers, K., Probst, R., Rief, L. (2007). *Adolescent literacy: Turning promise into practice.* Portsmouth, NH: Heinemann.

Delpit, L. (1995). *Other people's children: Cultural conflict in the classroom.* New York: The New Press.

Dutro, E., & Zenkov, K. (2008). Urban students testifying to their own stories: Talking back to deficit perspectives. In Y. Kim et. al. (Eds.), *57th Yearbook of the National Reading Conference.* (pp. 172–186). National Reading Conference.

Flake, G. (2004). *Who am I without him?: Short stories about girls and the boys in their lives.* New York: Hyperion.

Franklin, W. (2000). Students at promise and resilient: A historical look at risk. In M. Sanders (Ed.), *Schooling students placed at risk: Research, policy, and practice in the education of poor and minority adolescents.* (pp. 3–16). Mahwah, NJ: Lawrence Erlbaum Associates.

Franzak, J. (2006). *Zoom*: A review of the literature on marginalized adolescent readers, literacy theory, and policy implications. *Review of Educational Research, 76* (2), 209–248.

Gee, J. (2005). *An introduction to discourse analysis theory and method.* New York: Routledge.

Hamovich, B. (1997). *Staying after school: At-risk students in a compensatory education program.* Westport, CE; Praeger Publications.

Moje, E. (2000). "To be part of the story": The literacy practices of gangsta adolescents. *Teachers College Record, 102* (3), 651–690.

Moll, L., et. al. (1992). Funds of knowledge for teaching: Using a qualitative approach to connect homes and classrooms. *Theory into Practice, 31* (1), 132–141.

O'Brien, D. (2001). "At-risk" adolescents: Redefining competence through the multiliteracies of intermediality, visual arts, and representation. *Reading Online, 4* (11).

Richman, J., Rosenfeld, L., & Bowen, G. (1998). Social support for adolescents at risk of school failure. *Social Work, 43* (4), 309–323.

Rief, L. (2007). Writing commonsense matters. In K. Beers, R. Probst, and L. Rief (Eds.), *Adolescent literacy: Turning promise into practice.* (pp. 189–212). Portsmouth, NH: Heinemann.

Triplett, C. (2007). The social construction of "struggle": Influences of school literacy contexts, curriculum, and relationships. *Journal of Literacy Research, 39* (1), 95–126.

Vogt, M. (2004/2005). President's message: Fitful nights. *Reading Today,* 22 (3), 6.

Wise, B. (2009). Adolescent literacy: The cornerstone of student success. *Journal of Adolescent & Adult Literacy, 52* (5), 369–375.

Chapter Three

"If I Feel Like Writing, It's Easier": Adolescent Girls' Discourse Models of Writing in and out of School

Narrative Profile of Veronica

Veronica joined the writing group in the latter half of her seventh grade year. My initial impression of Veronica was that she was athletic, quiet, and serious about expressing herself through writing. In seventh grade, Veronica's chiseled cheekbones and shy grin illuminated an otherwise unadorned face and preference for a no-nonsense ponytail hairstyle. Veronica was also socially removed from the cliques present in the group. She knew all of the girls in the group, but she did not claim any of them as friends or enemies in other settings. During her first day in the writing group, Veronica created the following piece:

The True Color

Do you know what you are? Do you know your own culture? Well I do, people say that your suppose to be so proud of your culture, but what happens when people make fun of your for you or judge you. Sometimes it's just one of those situations that you don't know what to do. But when you think about it, it's life, like they say life isn't perfect, so why try to make it.

One day when I went to go stay with my friend Abby she told me if I wanted to go help her deliver her papers around her block. See she was a delivery girl, she delivered newspapers around her neighborhood. So me and her went walking around her block to go give the people their papers. Ding, dong! We had rang the door bell when a caucasian woman had opened the door, she was dressed in a tan silky shirt with dark blue jeans. She looked very nice but that's what we thought.

"What do you kids want?" she said in a mean voice. Abby had told her that we were here to sell her, her weekly newspaper. When she told us that she wouldn't buy it from us because we were Hispanic. That's what got Abby and I the most. We hated that she was raced to us, but that was okay because we knew that our color was who we were.

In this writing Veronica wrote somewhat philosophically about a startling experience with racism and concluded quickly with a child-like statement about color that echoed the title of the piece in both critical and magnanimous tones. As I became better acquainted with Veronica, I noticed she often held both a critical stance simultaneously with a resigned sense of the inevitability of larger oppressive social patterns as if cradling one view in each hand at an equal distance from her gaze.

Veronica routinely asserted critical observations about race and gender roles as she wrote about her experiences in the writing group. By eighth grade, however, Veronica began to adopt a more feminized gender persona both on her *MySpace* page and through discussions of dating and gender roles in the group. In eighth grade, Veronica began to wear makeup, nail polish, highlights in her hair, and bright plastic jewelry color-coordinated to match her sleek T-shirts. In eighth grade, Veronica transformed from a quiet, plain-faced tennis player into a sparkly, fashion-conscious teen balancing on the threshold of the cafeteria as she scoured the halls for boys she knew with her friends. In eighth grade Veronica dated the same boy for five months. This worried her mother, who subsequently cautioned Veronica against sneaking out of her bedroom window to meet her boyfriend as she had done at the same age and become pregnant. "I know you. You're just like I was at your age," Veronica quoted her mother with a tone possessing both warning and camaraderie. Veronica shrugged off such advice from her mother, however, because she did not believe life had been so bad for her mom. She also believed she was too smart to get pregnant as a teenager.

Veronica's father lived in the same city, but had never acknowledged her as his child, so she knew of him from a great distance even though in reality he lived only a few miles away from her. Of this relationship Veronica stated, "Sometimes like it hurts me to know that he's not around but then at other times it doesn't bother me because I know I have other people to love me," then added, "A mom is more better because she's the one who gave me life." In fact, with one exception all of the other girls in the group described their relationships with their mothers in similar quasi-peer/confidant ways and described relationships with their fathers as possessing varying degrees of physical, psychological, and emotional distance. Because Veronica did not know anything about her father other than his name, she had the most distanced relationship with her father of all the girls in the writing group.

Veronica was also the only girl in the group who viewed text messaging as a form of writing, largely because she once wrote a poem in a text message that got forwarded around her circle of friends and family and was eventually returned to her in a text message. This acknowledgment of her writing by an authentic audience made her feel a sense of legitimacy and pride. She also described text messaging as "starting a conversation" that could lead to writing in other venues.

Veronica stated she wrote every day to organize her life. Writing for personal purposes such as this helped her cope with her feelings and created a safe place to work through problems and express emotions. "Writing helps you make your way through life and stick up for yourself," she explained. When I asked Veronica about the difference between writing in school and writing in the Third Space writing group she stated, "In English class, the teacher picks a topic" and explained she had to devote a great deal of time thinking "towards" the chosen topic before writing. "In writing group, thoughts start coming to us. Something I'm ready for outside of school. I mess around with words and write it down. Or, if I'm going through something." For Veronica writing offered a kind of linguistic and intellectual play. It was also intricately tied to situations in her life. Indeed, writing as a way to navigate and understand one's emotions was the most significant reason all of the girls in the group cited for engaging in writing constructed of their own initiative.

Research on Adolescent Girls' Writing Practices

Several common purposes, roles, topics, and conditions have been discovered in previous studies conducted over both the in-school and out-of-school writing practices of adolescent girls. One of the most common recurring findings is the manner in which adolescent girls often organize out-of-school writing experiences through collective social systems. More specifically, adolescent girls' writing is often collaborative or dialogic in nature and perpetuated through their participation in various social affinity groups and Discourse communities (Finders, 1997; Guzzetti & Gamboa, 2004; Skinner, 2007). Additionally, researchers have discovered there are particular social languages, codes, and expectations for writing established by girls in the various Discourse communities and literacy practices they engage in, such as text messaging, handwritten notes passed during class, signing yearbooks, peer review during writer's workshop, and creating acceptable topics for a zine (Finders, 1997; Guzzetti & Gamboa, 2004). For instance, Styslinger (2008) found peer review of writing in a classroom environment for female adolescents is primarily about social positioning via "off task" behaviors that include attention to the other writers' feelings as well as deprecation of the self as a writer. Also, due in part to the coded nature of the writing and due in part to restrictive circulation practices, much of the writing adolescent girls initiate through their participation in various

Discourse communities is hidden entirely from broader audiences or relegated to a smaller subculture audience such as punk rock fans (Finders, 1997; Guzzetti & Gamboa, 2004).

With respect to writing topics, Hunt (1995) found the adolescent girls in her classes wrote about personal experiences and relationships "involving family and close friends" with greater frequency than adolescent boys (p. 9). Other researchers have noted that both assimilation and resistance to traditional gender roles for females were a recurring theme in the writing of adolescent girls (Finders, 1997; Guzzetti & Gamboa, 2004; Hubbard, Barbieri, & Power, 1998; Hunt, 1995; Skinner, 2007). In terms of writing style, adolescent girls' writing has been described often as a hybrid of "sanctioned" (in-school) and "unsanctioned" (out-of-school) types of literacies (Finders, 1997; Guzzetti & Gamboa, 2004; Skinner, 2007). In developing "unsanctioned" forms of writing, adolescent girls have been found to draw on "mentor texts" from popular culture to construct writing and models about their gender, age, and ethnicity in out-of-school and as much as permissible in-school settings (Finders, 1997; Grote, 2006; Skinner, 2007). As part of this phenomenon, Grote (2006) noted at-risk adolescent girls often mimicked vernacular language use in their writing.

Although there has been a fair amount of research conducted over the writing practices of adolescent girls, transformative or meaningful writing instruction for adolescent girls (Hubbard, Barbieri, & Power, 1998) has not become a central concern of literacy pedagogy in schools or curriculum in teacher preparation programs across the United States. Furthermore, within the corpus of research on adolescent girls' writing, at-risk adolescent girls have received the least amount of attention. Even in the wake of a plethora of research devoted to adolescent literacy there remains a paucity of studies and policies specifically concerned with at-risk adolescent girls.

Taking a Wider View on Policy Mandates and Writing Pedagogy

In 2003, the National Commission on Writing in America's Schools and Colleges published a study entitled "The Neglected 'R': The Need for a Writing Revolution" detailing the lack of effective writing instruction taking place in schools in the United States (Retrieved March 16, 2010 from http://www.writingcommission.org/prod_downloads/writingcom/neglectedr .pdf). While the authors voiced a general failing of K-12 schools to provide effective writing instruction, particular concern was cited about the quality of writing instruction occurring with adolescents. In the commission's study, the authors noted adolescents have been deemed to be disproportionately limited in their instructional experiences and exposure to writing. Similar concerns have been echoed by writing pedagogy experts in discussions of adolescent literacy (e.g., Romano, 2000, 2007; Gallagher, 2006; Murray, 2007; Rief, 2007) and addressed in policy statements from learned societies in the field of literacy education (e.g., NCTE). Of such neglect, the National Commission on Writing in America's Schools and Colleges noted in their report:

> When education was a private good, available to only a small elite in the United States, grammar, rhetoric, and logic were considered to be the foundation on which real learning and self-knowledge were built. . . . To reap the full benefits of the great democratization of learning in the United States, these three elements should still be pillars of learning. (p. 9)

The findings from the commission's report suggest the United States educational system is not far from returning to such a time when only a few students have access to writing instruction. The most recent National Assessment of Educational Progress (NAEP) data points to a need for better writing instruction as well.

The 2007 NAEP data on writing scores with eighth grade and twelfth grade students has drawn both praise and criticism as an indicator of the writing instruction taking place in K-12 schools (Institute of Education Sciences, Retrieved May 21, 2010, from http://nces.ed.gov/nationsreportcard /pdf/main2007/2008468.pdf). On the positive side, trends in this data show an increase in students reaching a basic level of writing. For eighth grade students in 2007 the average writing score was three percentage points higher than in 2002 and six percentage points higher than in 1998. The percentage of students performing at or above the *Basic* level increased from 85 percent in 2002 to 88 percent and was also higher than in 1998. The percentage of students performing at or above the *Proficient* level was higher than in 1998 but showed no significant change since 2002. For twelfth grade students in 2007 the average writing score was five percentage points higher than in 2002 and three percentage points higher than in 1998. The percentage of twelfth grade students performing at or above the *Basic* level increased from 74 percent in 2002 to 82 percent and was also higher than in 1998. The percentage of students performing at or above the *Proficient* level was higher than in 1998 but showed no significant change since 2002. Two percent of eighth grade students and one percent of twelfth grade students received an advanced score in 2007. This score was the same in 2002.

On the negative side, these trends in test scores seem encouraging until one considers NAEP's definitions for the categories used to evaluate student writing and the fact that the positive gains in test scores since both 2002 and 1998 occurred primarily at the *Basic* level. A *Basic* level of writing is described by NAEP as writing that "denotes partial mastery of prerequisite knowledge and skills that are fundamental for proficient work at a given grade" (2010, p. 6). The *Proficient* level is described as representing "solid academic performance. Students reaching this level have demonstrated competency over challenging subject matter" (p. 6). Advanced writing is described as "superior performance" (p. 6). The 2007 NAEP writing scores indicate eighth grade females outscored their male counterparts on average by twenty points. This data also indicates eighth graders receiving free or reduced lunch scored twenty-five percentage points below students not eligible to receive free and reduced lunch. No statistical data combining family income level and gender is available from the analysis published by NAEP.

In response to national concerns about the quality of secondary-level education, policy has recently been enacted to address the gap between adolescents' writing skills upon graduating from high school and college expectations for writing through the formulation of College and Career Readiness Standards. These standards have been emerging across the nation during the past two years. At present, a nationwide common core of College and Career Readiness Standards is in the final stages of development. Texas adopted a set of College and Career Readiness Standards in 2008 designed to ensure all graduating seniors possessed the "knowledge and skills necessary to succeed in entry-level community college and university courses" (The Texas Higher Education Coordinating Board, Retrieved April 7, 2010, from http://www.txccrs.org/downloads/CCRS_Standards.pdf, p. iii). In Texas, College and Career Readiness Standards for Writing consist of a description of the organizing components of writing followed by five examples of performance indicators. The components are predicated upon a philosophy of teaching writing as a process and demonstrate fairly basic goals for rhetorical awareness of writing events and academic expectations for writing proficiency.[1]

In Texas, there is also a state mandated writing exam for fourth and seventh grade students. Additionally, tenth and eleventh grade students take an English language arts exam that contains both reading comprehension and writing components. The writing test for seventh grade consists of two sample writings students must edit for grammatical accuracy via multiple choice questions followed by writing an original composition over a prompt such as "Write a composition about something that made you proud" (Retrieved from the Texas Education Agency website, May 16, 2010 from

---

[1] Please see Appendix B for a copy of the Texas College and Career Readiness Standards for Writing.

http://222.tea.state.tx.us/index3.asp?id=4118&menu_id=793#writing.). The tenth and eleventh grade English language arts tests include reading passages with multiple choice questions, "open-ended" questions about the reading material, a revision/editing multiple choice section, and an original composition.

Although these standards and exams are designed to ensure student success with writing, they did little in the way of improving interest in academic writing for the adolescent girls in the writing group. In interviews, the girls cited six venues for writing they had participated in as middle school students: personal journals created at home and rarely if ever shared with anyone, notes written to friends and circulated subversively and often pervasively during school, various types of *MySpace* postings, test preparation–oriented writing tasks required in school, text messaging (although only one of the girls viewed texting as writing), and the writing composed during their participation in the Third Space writing group. Of these six venues for writing, school writing was the least preferred type of writing as well as the least memorable for the girls. The writing required for school and specifically for test preparation seemed always to be an irrelevant chore and in ways even an obstacle to the girls' writing development.

Discourse Models of School Writing

In interviews and discussions with the girls, the terminology or philosophy referenced in writing standards such as the ones governing the state mandated test or the state's College and Career Readiness Standards were never expressed. In fact, the girls presented very limited descriptions and Discourse models of the writing instruction they received in school. Gee defined Discourse models as the "largely unconscious theories" individuals hold about "texts and the world" that shape their actions (p. 71). Discourse models are "images" and "storylines" of "taken-for-granted assumptions about what is 'typical' or 'normal'" (p. 72). Gee also explained Discourse models are revealed through one's use of language, tools, texts, nonverbal behaviors, and other kinds of artifacts to describe life experiences understood through the lens of social and cultural groups (p. 37 & 38).

In interviews at the conclusion of the study, I asked the girls about their experiences with writing in school. Uniformly the girls responded that writing in school was about developing teacher directed topics. Grammar figured into their discussions of school writing in the ways the girls described test preparation worksheets that involved correcting grammar mistakes in sample prose. The girls also shared a few practice compositions written in their English class. For instance, Tia shared an example of writing entitled "The Move" she had completed in preparation for her seventh grade state mandated writing exam over the prompt, "Write about a time when something unexpected happened."

The Move

> I will never forget the day like just a other day I came home from school when and I walk in the door I saw my mom on the phone and when she got off she told me and my sister to pack are stuff or the most import stuff that we need. I asked my mom why but there was no answer.

> Later that day when we got done packing we put all are stuff in the van it seemed like we driven a million miles then we stop and I looked out the window and we are at my grandmothers house. Ones again I asked my mom why did we leave home but still no answer later that night when I was unpacking I took a quick glance at the TV the news as on I could not believe what I saw the house or what was left of it someone had put I on fire over a fight that my mom had at work and my mom was informed about it and got us out as soon as she could. This made me so mad but thankful that we got away.

Tia's response to the practice exam was a partially fictional account of her mother's dramatic rescue of her family from a violent altercation with a co-worker. Even though Tia's essay contained a sense of beginning-middle-and-end story structure with active verbs and details, she reported not being very invested in this essay. In fact, all of the girls described the test preparation writing they did as little more than a dull shade of meaningless. In spite of Tia's dislike of school writing, she passed her state writing exam a few months after she composed this essay. Thus, meeting the passing require-ments of the exam did not insure Tia's (or the other girls') engagement with writing.

A year after their participation in the writing group, I met with four girls for lunch to talk about their perspectives on writing in school since their participation in the group. Through the course of our conversation, I asked them if they felt the writing they did in the Third Space writing group had helped them with their seventh grade state mandated standardized writing test and/or the writing assignments they completed for school in sixth, seventh, and eighth grade. Their response about the writing group's effect on their writing was unanimously positive, but they added a couple of key points to bear in mind: (1) they could not remember what they wrote about on their seventh grade writing exam or how they had been instructed in writing to prepare for this exam in school beyond practice exams and grammar worksheets and (2) they claimed they had been required to write one essay their entire eighth grade year. By contrast, the girls had vivid memories of the narratives and poetry they had written during their participation in the writing group.

Of the solitary writing assignment in their eighth grade English class, the four girls described the writing as a fluke prompted by their teacher's personal tragedy. They explained their English teacher's son had died suddenly and in her grief she had asked her students to write about an object that was special to them since one particular object of her son's had become special to her upon his death. Isabel and Felicia spoke about how they selected a meaningful topic for this assignment. Isabel wrote about a gold necklace her grandfather had given her, bearing his astrological sign, when he was still alive. Felicia wrote about a picture of her dad depicting happier memories than the last time she had seen him for a visitation in which he spent most of the time sitting in his car with his girlfriend "smoking a lot; smoking really bad [drugs]" while she and her brother were stuck in his house eating cereal and drinking Coca Cola. Given this prompt and opportunity to write for a personal purpose Isabel and Felicia opted to write about emotionally charged and relevant topics for them. The girls reported connecting to this writing assignment, but complained that after this experience the writing assignments had ceased. In summary, the girls held the following Discourse models for writing assigned in school: (1) topics for writing were almost entirely determined by the teacher, (2) writing to support test preparation dominated their writing instruction, and (3) writing connected to their real-life experiences and feelings was extremely rare.

Discourse Models of Out-of-School Writing

Purposes for out of school writing were invariably tied to the girls' emotions about their life experiences and being in a particular frame of mind conducive to writing. In interviews, the girls stated they wrote when they felt sad, angry, lonely, or bored. The following excerpt from a discussion with three of the girls in the writing group illustrates the role of emotions (and music that enhanced their emotional state of mind) in shaping the girls' writing.

ML: As you think about your future, what are your goals for yourselves as writers?

Amber: I wanna write a book.

Felicia: I know it's like when you write it makes you wanna gather up all your things.
Amber: And put them in a book.

Felicia: Yeah.

ML: It makes you want to write more? The more writing you do, the more writing you want to do?
[Felicia and Amber nodded their heads in agreement.]

Isabel: But, I have to be in the mood. If I'm not, then I'm not going to write.

ML: What helps you get into the mood to write?

Isabel: Being happy. Hearing music.

Amber: Yeah.

Isabel: Yeah if there's something I like to hear like a lot of then I can write all day if I want.

ML: What kind of music? Music with words or music without words—like when you hear lyrics does it mess up your writing?

Amber: When I hear lyrics it helps me more.

Isabel: Yeah like my favorite one is "Baby" by Ashanti.

ML: Why? Because it puts you in a good mood?

Isabel: Yeah. It always puts me in a good mood. The other one is "Do What You Want."

ML: Ok, so what about when you're sad? Because some of you said in your interviews last year that sometimes you write because you feel sad.

Felicia: Because it takes out all your anger.

Amber: I know!

Felicia: When I'm writing and I'm mad I put on some like music that like I'm so mad I just want to break this pencil!

In addition to connecting out-of-school writing to emotional responses to their life experiences, out-of-school writing was created around purposes for public and private writing. The girls were keenly aware of distinctions between public and private writing. In this manner, out-of-school writing was also tightly dictated by the Discourse communities in which the girls participated. Forums such as *MySpace* permitted the girls to work through their feelings in coded messages posted publicly but primarily accessible to their socially delineated peer networks. When angry, sad, elated, or bored the girls could write messages to peers in a coded language to express their feelings. Much of this coded writing about their feelings occurred on *MySpace* through their "mood" and "status" updates. Similarly, the girls described the ways they often worked out new hierarchies of social power on the rankings of their "friends list." This kind of coded public and thus to some extent private writing helped them express feelings, create new configurations of peer networks and identities, and stick up for friends. They also wrote messages on their friends' *MySpace* pages for the same purposes. For instance, several girls talked about writing such messages in order to "dis" boys or other girls who had hurt a friend's feelings.

Public Writing

Engaging in public writing required a degree of risk for the girls in the group. Beyond quietly asserting social power through such writing, the girls also took risks in public writing through experimentation with text. Writing occurring outside of school settings in public forums provided opportunities for the girls to create writing that pulled at the seams of traditional academic expectations for writing. Departures from the norm were not mistakes; they were new trends and new rules for writing. Improvisation and hybridized usage were valued. For instance, consider the structure of the following message posted to Veronica's *MySpace* page: "gEt OfF mYsPacE LIL sIStEr . . . . . iTs LaTe 4 yOn tOo bE uP . . . . .lOl . . ." In this manner, like the middle-class, European American adolescent girls creating zines in Guzzetti and Gamboa's (2004) study, the girls in this study used "literacy as a creative and artistic process and a way to rebel against the formal practices learned in school" (p. 426).

Although the writing the girls did on *MySpace* and to some extent in the writing group often did not emulate the expectations for conventions of academic writing and in this manner was rebellious, the girls' examination of marginalization and oppression in their writing was primarily nascent. Criticisms of their life experiences were often sequestered away from their public writing and would emerge publicly in the writing group only when they felt a level of trust with the other group members and me. Even when they made observations about the ways boys treated them (such as humping against them as they stood in line for food in the cafeteria) or how they hated the way their stepfathers behaved they rarely critiqued such behavior. Beyond voicing a mild complaint, they generally acquiesced to an expectation that this is the way life is for girls. Part of this social tone was due to the public forum. While the public nature of *MySpace* and the writing group allowed for new forms of creativity and expression, at the same time the public context of such forums served to inhibit social criticism. This kind of commentary was more often expressed in the girls' private or "hidden" writing.

Hidden Writing

In discussions about writing practices beyond writing in school and the writing group, the girls all stated they engaged in some form of writing they kept hidden from audiences beyond themselves. In this manner, the audience as self was a recurring Discourse model for their out-of-school writing. Such venues for hidden writing usually included diaries and journals kept locked away from parents, peers, and teachers. I observed the tentacles of hidden writing in the girls' composing on several occasions when they would type a paragraph of prose on a computer screen, realize I was standing behind them reading it, and decide to erase it before I could persuade them to let me save their writing. Over time the girls became used to my reading writing they wanted to keep to themselves, but they still often erased their words after letting me read them. On one such occasion, Kecia showed me her writing, put her finger to her lips, silently whispered "shhhh," and glanced at one of her friends seated at the next computer indicating she did not want her friend to see what she had composed. Kecia wanted me to read what she had written about a boy she had a crush on, but did not want her friend to have access to this information. I smiled and nodded silently to acknowledge my understanding of her request. At moments like this, I realized my role with the girls had taken on a unique hue. I was not so much a teacher or parental adult figure who would judge their personal thoughts, but rather someone who could be trusted to be let in on secrets that even their best friends were not privy to. In this manner, I came to see my stance as a key component to the Third Space environment. I was both a writing coach and a confidant to whom the girls began to turn for advice in their writing as well as the challenges they faced with boys, peers, and parents.

Like the girls in Guzzetti and Gamboa's (2004) study, all of the girls stated they preferred not to share their writing with their mothers. Felicia described hiding her journal in a box in a vent on the floor of her room with a rug over the top of it. She stated she hid her journal from her mom to keep her mom from reading writing about how angry she felt towards her stepfather. Similarly, writing created in the writing group was often kept away from mothers too. Samantha made everyone tear her writing out of a book of the girls' writing I put together for them in order to keep her mom from reading about her boyfriend, exclaiming "My mom will kill me!" The girls primarily hid their writing from friends and parents because of the personal information it contained. In this manner, hidden writing was fundamentally a place for the girls to examine secrets, rehearse social roles (e.g., being a girlfriend), and contemplate decisions *privately*. For example, Kiara captured the necessity of keeping secrets in a piece entitled "Secrets" in which she used writing to help her work up the courage to tell a few trusted people her secret.

Secrets

Secrets are things people tell other people. These aren't just any facts or comments, these are things that some one says to another person that they don't want anybody to know about. You may think you can tell anybody these secrets, but you can't.

You have to be bale to TRUST the person you tell. Trust is hard to have especially when you are a teen. I only have one person that I trust, only one person I can tell almost any thing to. Her name is Shayla.

Well you see I have this big secret that I feel I can't tell anybody about because I don't know what they are going to think about the subject. This secret I have needed to come out, so it did because I told shayla. Only her though nobody else I'm too scared to trust the people I used to because they've let out some of my secrets. So now I kind of limit myself with people. I could never really open up to many people like I use to.

Well this passage is mainly to inform you to have trust before telling secrets to many people. The person that you can really, really trust is yourself. But for my moment of wisdom "Trust yourself before you can trust others."

In this piece Kiara danced around telling the secret that she later confided to me privately but could not risk opening up for other audiences by putting it into print in the writing group. The process of writing about telling her secret, however, helped her work through her fears of actually telling a socially risky secret.

Key Components to the Composing Process in a Third Space Setting

When I asked Isabel and Felicia whether they felt they had grown as writers through their participation in the Third Space writing group, Felicia commented she had learned to write with more details and "describing more." She added, "The more you've been through, the more you notice and have to write about." Isabel stated, "Now I write about more emotional stuff, more deep thoughts. I think I'm growing mature more faster than most people. What I used to think is funny is stupid." Both Felicia and Isabel stated they did not get caught up in social "drama" with their friends as they've had more practice with writing but rather took on more of an observer role, which allowed them to notice more things and this noticing led to their writing with more details. They also stated they had learned to think more about the reader's perspective—what people want to know and think about their writing. I asked how they thought they had developed this skill in light of the fact that I offered minimal amounts of direct writing instruction. Isabel stated without hesitation, "You were there for us emotionally." She explained my reading her work and giving her feedback on what was "good" and offering ideas for her writing helped her become a better writer. These observations were offered at the conclusion of their third year in the writing group. Beyond these perspectives offered by the girls, I discovered several aspects of Third Space writing that provided unique support for the writing development of at-risk girls.

Taking Risks in Writing

A key component to the success of the writing in this project was the process the girls went through of learning to take risks as writers. Taking risks served as a creative and emotional bridge between hidden and public writing. Following one week where Amber had written about being molested and feeling suicidal, Felicia had written about her dad's drug addiction, and Kiara had written about her stepdad's alcoholism, I asked the girls about the risks they had taken as writers in sharing these stories. They readily acknowledged the personal risks of this kind of writing and stated they felt "ok" about taking this risk because they all understood each other's lives. This level of trust took time to develop in the group but was an important ingredient in the girls' beginning to develop positive views of their writing ability.

Writing Process

Topics generated for writing in the writing group were almost always spontaneous in nature. The pre-writing strategies such as brainstorming the girls engaged in were brief explorations—usually guided by my prompting. The composing process of the girls', including elements of pre-writing activities, peer review, and editing, was condensed in the writing group and in the descriptions they gave me of writing they did in other settings. Other than the informal writing conferences they engaged in with me, revision was virtually nonexistent beyond cursory editing. The girls were also extremely sensitive about receiving criticism over their writing. They hated writing for teachers because of this and mistrusted peer feedback as well. In fact, criticism was cited as an obstacle to writing because they felt people judged them for what they wrote or for their use of grammar. Like Styslinger's

(2008) study examining the function of gender in adolescents' peer review discussions, such peer commentary was highly indicative of the girls' personal relationships with one another. Thus, peer feedback put the girls in a vulnerable social position.

One afternoon after three years of participating in the writing group, Felicia paused in her typing to ask Isabel to read the title of a piece Felicia was beginning to compose on the computer. Felicia had been experimenting with different colors, capitalization patterns, and fonts with her title. After settling on one version, she leaned over to Isabel and asked, "What does this say?" Isabel responded, "Nervousness." Felicia said, "Just checking to make sure it's readable." This was one of the few times I observed the girls spontaneously request feedback from one another about their writing.

Initially, the group attempts at writer's workshop ended up in rude comments from peers. It took two years to get to a place where the girls could begin to respond to one another's writing without making fun of each other. Moreover, writer's workshop did not prompt revision beyond superficial editing such as correcting a spelling error. The girls primarily relied on spell check and feedback from me to correct mechanical errors in their writing. Consequently, with peer feedback and revision barely visible, writer's workshop was mostly about the girls giving voice to their writing. Even so, this process of making writing public was an important first step in the girls' beginning to engage in elements of writing process theory (e.g., revision) and beginning to view themselves as writers in school settings where critique was prevalent.

Sense of Audience

On several occasions throughout the writing group I asked the girls who they had in mind as they wrote both within the group and within other settings (e.g., personal diaries, *MySpace*, school). This question usually drew shrugs and "what-do-you-mean?" requests for clarification. After explaining my question, the girls offered responses of "no one" or "myself" or "my friends" or even once in a while "my mom." Sense of audience was constructed around the dichotomy of private and public writing. The audience for public writing consisted of peers and significant adults (e.g., youth minister, aunt, mom). The audience for private writing consisted of self and sometimes nonjudgmental/supportive adults (e.g., the C.I.S. campus coordinator, their aunt, me). Although the girls did not consciously consider their audience until prompted, unconsciously this writing was greatly shaped by thoughts of potential audiences. Self-initiated writing was often hampered by concerns about others reading their work and a desire to keep personal writing hidden. The girls tended to resist the idea of engaging an audience in an effort to protect themselves from potential criticism. Assertively addressing an audience as a writer was a slowly evolving process that took a great deal of time for the girls to warm up to. After three years in the writing group, Kiara ventured beyond composing narratives for herself and her best friends. At the end of her eighth grade year, Kiara wrote the following piece one afternoon in the writing group. It was one of the final three pieces she composed.

Is it?

Is it so bad to want things? Is it bad to want to hang out with different people? Is it so bad to want lots of people to talk to? Is it good to hate things or is it wrong?

These questions asked above are questions very few people can answer correctly. I myself don't have the answer. But I do know one person that does. He can answer you questions in the most bizarre way. He is who I like to call god. Lots of people don't like to speak of him but why. Is it because they are too embarrassed or is it because they don't believe in him? Well I know this girl that told me a story about this one guy who didn't no about god. Here's the story . . . .

Ok so this boy named David used to sit with her in many classes that she had. She never talked to him but new that something about him was missing. David always did bad things. My friend said that David didn't no about god; she said that she wished she should've told him more about god and Jesus, and the bible. You may ask why but it's because . . . David got really really drunk and high and got into a car accident. Later that day David was pronounced dead . . . .

After remarking how powerful her story was because of the topic and the device she employed of switching speakers (and fonts) to create narrative texture through multiple perspectives, I asked Kiara who her audience was. Her face became still as she thought for a few moments and then responded with confidence, "My uncle. He's in rehab—or a place like rehab where you go instead of going to jail. He got real lucky." Then, she turned back to the computer screen, changed the font to the first one she used and added:

I tell you this story because I don't want the same thing to happen to you. I want you to know what the right path to take is. I believe that the right path is to follow god's ways.

Kiara asked me if she could print out several copies of this paper to give to family members and mail to her uncle. She also wrote a cover letter to her uncle in a separate document explaining the purpose for the narrative she composed. Such specific and conscious attention to an audience was rare beyond the primary audience of self and peers that were typically referenced by the girls.

Developing an Identity as a Writer

When I asked the girls about their views of themselves as writers, most of the girls responded with a statement that tied writing to their sense of self. For example, Simone stated, "It [writing] reflects who you are." Because meaningful writing was emotionally and personally connected to their lives, a positive writing identity was intricately tied to the response they received from others about their writing. In fact, several of the girls also equated the quality of their writing to their ability to evoke an emotional response in others. It was as if they believed real writers had an *approving* audience. By the end of the writing project, all of the girls were on the verge of sharing more of their writing with others and thus viewing themselves as writers. However, every day this identity hung in a delicate balance that could be easily disrupted by an adult's (e.g., a teacher or parent) comments or peer ridicule. So, the girls largely kept their writing hidden in deleted paragraphs drafted in the writing group, tucked away in a carefully stashed book in their room, or couched in private text messages filled with acronyms. Their fear of facing a reader's criticism was the phenomenon that most profoundly inhibited their identity as writers.

In order to develop a positive identity as a writer, the girls in the writing group needed a safe space to write in which they felt free from peer and adult criticism. They needed an environment where they could isolate themselves psychologically and focus on writing without peer distraction. They needed to learn to value their own writing. They also needed to write their way through the stress of entering into adolescent social expectations and gendered roles. In this manner, introspection and reflection were also necessary experiences in developing a writing identity.

Concluding Vignette: A Turning Point

After several weeks of unprompted writing time, I pulled the group together in a circle to read and respond to drafts of one another's writing that the girls had selected for a book I was putting together for them. Amid competition for privacy in the library where another advisory group was watching a film on learning to feel empathy for others, the girls moved their chairs into a circle and began to navigate the delicate topography of giving and receiving feedback on their writing. After responding to the first five pieces, we turned to Tara's writing in the packet. Now in the eighth grade, Tara had been in the group since it started as a sixth grader and had instigated more fights and uttered more mean comments to her peers than any other girl in the group. Tara was one of two females in the school the girls described as a bully. By the eighth grade, however, the fights she engaged in were becoming less frequent. Tara also began to sustain her focus on composing text for longer periods of time during the writing group. The piece of writing she selected captured a shift from writing about a distant "sexy" pop star icon to someone she had known. The following is an excerpt from the workshop:

Erica: Who's Katie?

Tara: My aunt.

Erica: [Referring to the next piece of writing in the packet.] Oh, this is yours?

ML: Okay are we ready to look at Tara's [piece of writing]?

Erica: [inaudible]

Tara: No, it's not. It's mine.

Erica: [inaudible]

Tara: I didn't. I forgot to put my name on it.

ML: Uh oh, that was a big typo referring to my editorial work.

Erica: Is this your Aunt Sugar [inaudible]?

Tara: No, she's white.

Erica: Oh.

[Tara giggles.]

ML: Ok, Tara, you ready?

Tara: Oh, no I don't want to read this!

Erica: Ooh, let me read! Can I read?

Tia: I'll read it!

Tara: Okay! [Begins reading her piece.]
I miss the way, I miss the way, um, you used to make me smile every time I would go to the house how I would always be with you. I know it is, it was your time to go and

now you, you are better and free from the disease that you have been fighting for two years. The thing that hurts me the most that I didn't [correcting herself] um, wait, since, uh, well, it's supposed to be *I didn't see you. Wait. I don't know what it's supposed to be. I didn't since, I didn't since you were diagnosed*
Simone: I didn't see you since you were diagnosed with cancer!

Tara: [Reading.] *with cancer but I never stop praying for you and how I never got a chance to say goodbye.*

Tia: [Playfully.] There's no way you wrote this! I cannot believe you wrote this!

[Several girls laughing at Tia's joke.]

ML: Okay so, let's all tell Tara something we liked about this writing. Erica.

Erica: Oh, I wasn't raising my hand I was just going like this. [Makes the motion again with her hand.]

[Several girls laugh.]

ML: You don't want to say something that you liked?

[Pause.]

Erica: I liked it because it reminded me of Hannah Montana. I liked this because it reminded me of the Hannah Montana song. [Begins singing.]

ML: Is that the song? Is that one of her songs?

Tara: No.

ML: Hannah Montana?

Tara: Yeah it talks about her grandpa.

Kiara: [Referring to Tara's writing.] It made me think of my Aunt Mary died of breast cancer.

Tara: Well my aunt—

ML: So you could really relate to her story.

Kiara: She already had her breasts removed, and she still got it back in the same place [inaudible].

Heather: Oh no.

ML: That's sad.

Simone: That is sad.

Kiara: [Softly.] I'm going to bring a poem.

Tara: My Aunt Katie, um, her mom died from the same thing, so it like runs in her family.

ML: That's sad. And, I think this is very powerful writing and you know what I like about it is that you're not joking around. Because you do a lot of joking around, and I thought this was really great for you as a writer specifically, Tara, to tell a story that was close to your heart. And, you weren't writing about, you know, some "sexy beast" because that's usually what you write about [laughs]. So, I was really proud of you for doing this last week. Okay what questions do you all want to ask Tara? What questions do you want to ask Tara about her writing?

Simone: Tara, why was that like your title? [Referring to the title, "Katie."] Like you wrote about her, your Aunt Sugar?

Tara: I didn't even know my Aunt Sugar.

Simone: Well I mean—

Tara: It's because she died, and whenever I wrote it, it was a year that, uh, she died December 1st.

ML: Oh it was on her date. What year did she die?

Tara: 2007.

ML: Okay, so a year ago. Exactly a year ago. What do you want to add to this writing, Tara?

Tara: I don't know. Nothing. I don't really have nothing to add.

ML: You edited yourself as you were reading it. Would you want to go back and edit some of your writing if you had the chance to?

Tara: Yes.

ML: Okay, good.

Although it took nearly two years to get to this point of sharing and respectfully responding to each other's writing, in this workshop the girls were beginning to engage one another as writers in a peer-editing process. Talking to one another about their writing—viewing one another as an audience for their writing—helped to collectively strengthen the girls' perceptions of themselves as writers.

Tara was also trying on a new narrative identity through her writing. Instead of using writing to sustain an identity ascribed to her by others, Tara presented an identity of the "self" she had created in opposition to the pervasive school views of herself as a bully and a mean clown (Yin, 2008, p. 1). In this Third Space setting it became possible for Tara to assert a new identity through both a written narrative and dialogue about her narrative. In fact, the narrative of her Aunt Katie was a "turning point" where Tara created a new literacy identity through the sense of self she presented as a writer. This workshop also captured the process of taking risks, learning to revise writing, and facing an audience the girls needed to go through in order to develop a positive academic view of themselves as writers. Even so, I wondered where the girls would go from this experience as writers. Would they continue to write on their own? Would hidden diary writing, *MySpace* postings, and infrequent school instruction in test preparation grammar and composition help these girls develop writing skills that could take them to college?

References

Finders, M. (1997). *Just girls: Hidden literacies and life in junior high*. New York: Teachers College Press.

Gallagher, K. (2006). *Teaching adolescent writers*. Portland, ME: Stenhouse.

Gee, J. (2005). An introduction to discourse analysis: Theory and method. New York, NY: Routledge.

Grote, E. (2006). Challenging the boundaries between school-sposored and venacular literacies: Urban indigenous teenage girls writing in an "at risk" programme. *Language and Education, 20* (6), 478492.

Guzzetti, B., & Gamboa, M. (2004). Zines for social justice: Adolescent girls writing on their own. *Reading Research Quarterly, 39* (4), 408436.

Hubbard, R., Barbieri, M., & Power B. (1998). *"We want to be known": Learning from adolescent girls*. York, ME: Stenhouse.

Hunt, S. (1995). Choice in the writing class: How do students decide what to write and how to write it? *Quarterly of the National Writing Project and the Center for the Study of Writing and Literacy, 17* (7), 1133.

Institute of Education Sciences . (2010). The nation's report card: Writing 2007. Author. Retrieved May 21, 2010 from http://nces.ed.gov/nationsreportcard/pdf/main2007/2009468.pdf

Murray, D. (2007). Teach writing your way. In K. Beers, R. Probst, and L. Rief (Eds.), *Adolescent literacy: Turning promise into practice*. (pp. 179188). Portsmouth, NH: Heinemann.

National Commission on Writing in America's Schools and Colleges. (2003). The neglected "r": The need for a writing revolution.

Rief, L. (2007). Writing commonsense matters. In K. Beers, R. Probst, and L. Rief (Eds.), *Adolescent literacy: Turning promise into practice*. (pp. 189212). Portsmouth, NH: Heinemann.

Romano, T. (2000). *Blending genre, altering style: Writing multigenre papers*. Portsmouth, NH: Heinemann.

———. (2007). Teaching writing from the inside. In K. Beers, R. Probst, and L. Rief (Eds.), *Adolescent literacy: Turning promise into practice*. (pp. 167178). Portsmouth, NH: Heinemann.

Skinner, E. (2007). "Teenage addiction": Adolescent girls drawing upon popular culture texts as mentors for writing in an after-school writing club. In D. Wells Rowe, R. Jimenez, D. Compton, D. Dickinson, Y. Kim, K. Leander, and V. Risko (Eds.), *56th Yearbook of the National Reading Conference* (pp. 345361). National Reading Conference.

Texas Education Agency. (2010). Grade 7 sample compositions. Author. Retrieved May 16, 2010 from http://222.tea.state.tx.us/index3.asp?id=4118&menu_id=793#writing.

The Texas Higher Education Coordinating Board (2008). College and career readiness standards. Author. Retrieved April 7, 2010 from http://www.txccrs.org/downloads/CCRSs_Standares.pdf.

Styslinger, M. (2008). Gendered performance during peer revision. *Literacy, Research and Instruction, 47*, 211228.

Yin, A. (2008). *Problematizing identity: Everyday struggles in language, culture, and education*. New York: Lawrence Erlbaum Associates.

Chapter Four

"My Poem to Someone I Loved and I Ruined It!": Dating Roles and Cultural Models of Gender

Narrative Profile of Kecia

Kecia was a quiet African American girl with dimples and short hair curled into a flip at the ends who was routinely referred to as "boy-crazy" by her peers. In seventh grade, Briana complained Kecia "stole" her nineteen-year-old boyfriend through a series of phone calls and text messages tapped into Briana's cell phone while they waited together for a ride home from school one afternoon. Rolling her eyes continually in humor and disgust, Kecia was in a tight-knit clique of friends who moved like a constant wall around her and whose social opinions she rarely contradicted beyond soft protests or a sullen gaze. "Cute" pictures of older siblings and their infant/toddler-aged children, her own baby picture, and a sprinkling of pictures of her hugging female friends filled her *MySpace* page. Although she was forbidden to date until she was fifteen, in seventh grade, Kecia had a boyfriend her parents did not know about because she met the boy secretly at various locations such as the mall and the three-dollar movie theater.

When Kecia was in seventh grade, we read the opening short story in Sharon Flake's (2005) book *Who Am I Without Him?* which details a nameless girl's relationship with an emotionally and physically abusive boyfriend. A few pages into the story, the female protagonist describes a fight with her boyfriend while waiting at the bus stop:

> I am loud like my mother. When I holler, you can hear me up and down the street and around the corner. So when I go off on Raheem, people across the street turn and stare. "You my man! What you doing looking at her for?" Raheem's hand smashes the words back into my mouth. "Girl, don't make me. . . ." I apologize just like my momma does when my daddy slaps her. Like Raheem's momma does too. Raheem says he's gonna forgive me this time. But I better check myself, 'cause he needs a cooperative woman. "Not a whole bunch of drama." (pp. 4–5)

Kecia sat riveted as I read this story aloud to the group and was unusually talkative at the conclusion about the ways boys treat girls in dating relationships. After making several observations about boyfriends, Tara effectively silenced Kecia from further commentary over the short story by accusing her of having "too much information about dating." Kecia's only response to this innuendo of sexual promiscuity was to glare in the direction of the table in front of her. In spite of such comments about her interest in and knowledge of dating boys from her friends, Kecia rarely contested these views. In seventh grade, Kecia quietly worked her way through relationships with friends, boys, and family. She challenged her father's rules about not dating. She tried on different mean attitudes with hostile gazes for the slightest infraction; she stepped into dating relationships with boys; and, she adhered herself to a clique.

In eighth grade, Kecia got braces, stopped rolling her eyes, wrote dreamily about marriage, smiled shyly when I talked to her about her writing, and began to break away from her wall of friends through more confident assertions. She chided Tara for telling Alicia she looked fat. Only a year earlier, she had ignored Tara's similar comment even though that time it had reduced Alicia to tears in the group. In eighth grade, Kecia's *MySpace* page still revolved around family pictures, but she also wrote encrypted messages to her current boyfriend with comments like "He's the one for me." At the end of eighth grade, she sang backup to another friend's rendition of the pop R&B recording artist Kelly Price's song "He Proposed" for the school talent show.

One mild November day, as she composed a piece about her family, Kecia quietly explained to my research assistant that her tenth grade boyfriend had cheated on her because she "wouldn't do what some girls do," which had abruptly ended their relationship. A few months later on Valentine's Day, I ran into Kecia and her clique of friends at the mall. Tara and Tia spoke with me while Kecia and Alicia kept their eyes glued on the thick stream of people passing before them, barely acknowledging my presence. Later, the group recounted an incident of Kecia's fighting with her boyfriend and making up with her ex-boyfriend during this visit to the mall.

Research Assistant: What are you going to write about?

Kecia: I don't know.

Tara: Her boyfriend Akeem.

Kecia: Akeem? Nope. Akeem? Nope. How about Monte? He bought me the candy.

Tara: Oh, she likes Monte because of the candy now so that was the good part.

Research Assistant: Kecia, what are you writing about?

Kecia: My exboyfriend.

Tia: Which one? Monte? Monte? Monte?

Kecia: Yeah. He was looking good on Saturday!

Tara: Eww Monte is ugly! He got a square head, he look like a bull dog! Miss. Okay, this boy named Monte he's a senior and used to go out with Kecia or whatever and he text Kecia. We were at the mall and he was like come here and leave the dogs behind. So me and Alicia went over there and we were like who are you calling a dog and he cussed me out first so I told him something and then Alicia told him something and then Monte told us something and then I was walking away—

Kecia: And then they looked at me and I was like I'm with my boyfriend now and they was like Kecia I ain't gonna fight your battles. I'm not going to fight your battles.

Even though all of the girls recounted these events in a humorous tone, there was an unresolved undercurrent of anger towards Kecia for taking up with an ex-boyfriend who insulted her friends.

A couple of days after this incident, Kecia wrote the following piece about her boyfriend:

My Rude Boyfriend

My boyfriend name is Akeem. He did not buy me something for Valentine's Day. I was mad then when I wanted 2 hug he act like he didn't want 2 hug me and he didn't want 2 kiss me. Than I look behind Akeem and I saw my ex and he was staring at me. Than he got up and walk off I think he was mad.

In this writing sample, Kecia offered a glimpse into her views on gender and dating roles. More specifically, she revealed expectations that male dating behavior hinges on physical affection, gift giving, and competition for a girl's attention.

In eighth grade Kecia kept secrets with her mother from her father about her weekend dating and series of adolescent boyfriends. In the writing group, her finished writing continued to focus on her large, extended family, which gave public primacy to her family membership and identity over her peer membership and identity. Privately, however, she drafted sentences about boys she liked on the computer such as "Derrick is cute" and then erased them before other girls in her clique saw what she had written, explaining to me that she wanted to keep her feelings about boys a secret from her friends. Even with the majority of her writing focusing on family membership, periodically Kecia also wrote about her struggle to find her footing along the emotional paths of dating relationships with boys. For instance, she wrote the following in writing group one afternoon:

> I saw my baby on Saturday. Can't talk about what we did. I finally kissed him and he kept hugging me and kissing me. My baby can do back flips. He was sad really sad when I left on Saturday. Then he text me as soon as I left I was happy man I am so happy wit him I'm in love wit him I hope we get married. His name is Devante Rayshon S------- my name would be Kecia? S------- I love him so much. My mom kind of likes him but I know she will when she meet him.

Kecia's writing about her boyfriends during seventh and eighth grade were reminiscent of all of the girls' writing about dating boys with respect to the gender identities that were formed through their imagined dating roles.

Gender Identity and Dating Roles

Feminist post-structural theories view gender as a socially constructed phenomenon where patriarchal ideologies and values are presented as "common sense" reasoning in order to "favour the interests of particular social groups" (Weedon, 1994, p. 77). Lewis (1993) viewed such common-sense values as being predicated upon hegemonic social systems or what Gee (2005) would refer to with less attention to issues of equity as Discourse communities. Lewis explained, "What counts as common sense is not an arbitrary matter but a matter of power. In the case of gender, while one does not negotiate one's biology, for certain one negotiates its meaning" (p. 82). Lather (1992) referred to such investigation into the meaning of gender as "critical inquiry" where one considers the ways lives "are mediated by systems of inequity" (p. 87). Lather added, "to do feminist research is to put the social construction of gender at the center of one's inquiry" (p. 91). Feminist post-structural theories help to explain the manner in which adolescent girls learn what it means to act and think in ways that identify them as females. In essence, adolescent girls' gender identities are formed through their participation in Discourse communities, fueling organizations and social structures such as school, family, peer groups, and the popular media (St. Pierre & Pillow, 2000).

In the past two decades little has changed for adolescent girls in terms of beliefs about gender norms and sexuality (Fine, 1992; Fine & McClelland, 2006). Adolescent girls are still the recipients of policies, curricula, and popular media that perpetuate cultural models of females as sexual victims whose best chances at happiness reside in dating/romantic relationships containing the double bind of boys who are both male protectors and male oppressors (Fine, 1992). Young adolescent girls—especially adolescent girls of color from low-income families—come of age in a society that has already vilified them as sexual hazards waiting to happen through teen pregnancy, sexually transmitted diseases, and high school attrition rates (Schultz, 2001; Tolman, 1996). Because young adolescents spend a great deal of time in school, these settings are key sites for replicating gender roles.

In the writing group, icons and norms surrounding heterosexual dating roles in the media and interactions with peers had a great impact on the girls' understanding of gender. In fact, such socially constructed notions of feminity and dating framed to a large extent the girls' views of their future aspirations, peer interactions, and gendered identities. Like many girls their age of varying socio-economic and ethnic backgrounds, the girls in this study had been inundated for years with messages of social norms surrounding gendered expectations for dating roles from the popular media, family, and peers (Finders, 1997; Pipher, 1994; Read, 2011; Sarroub, 2005). Like most adolescent girls across the United States, they also did not receive comprehensive sexuality education at school (Fine & McClelland, 2006). The virtually nonexistent sex education in the school along with the prevalence of abstinence only until marriage programs in the churches many of the girls attended served to render silent a large part of the girls' interactions with boys. The combination of ignoring male coercion, histories of sexual abuse, a need for accurate information about sex, and media messages about stereotypic dating roles made it difficult for the girls to form empowered gendered identities (Fine & McClelland, 2006).

More than two decades ago, Fine (1988) wrote of the need for comprehensive sexuality education for at-risk girls:

> Those most "at risk" of victimization through pregnancy, disease, violence, or harassment—all female students, low-income females in particular . . . are those most likely to be victimized by the absence of critical conversation in public schools. (p. 49)

Such critical conversations for the girls in the writing group were primarily relegated to informal encounters with family members, youth ministers, peers, and portrayals of dating from the popular media, all of which left the girls with a paucity of resources to draw on when encountering boys at school or in other settings away from the guidance of adults. I saw a need for such conversations on numerous occasions. For instance, when the pop and

R&B singer Chris Brown physically beat his pop and R&B singer girlfriend Rihanna and pictures of the battery were splashed all over the Internet and Hollywood gossip magazines, the girls unanimously sided with Chris Brown, explaining as they surfed the Internet for pictures of him to include with their writing that they felt he deserved someone better than Rihanna. Offering no sympathy for Rihanna's injuries, they critiqued her physical attractiveness by calling her "bald headed," overweight, and unable to "match" her clothes in a way that suggested her lack of physical beauty made the beating she experienced her fault and thus acceptable. Such media-induced conversations about dating were built on media-driven norms of physical beauty and the requirement of physical beauty in order to be desirable to boys. The almost callous, adamant nature of the girls' views about Rihanna highlighted a need to critically examine media images of dating. As Read (2011) noted of adolescent girls' fascination with celebrity role models, "the constructed images of such female celebrities represented more than anything else their own future ideal self-identity—who they would like to be when they grow up" (p. 4). In this case, Rihanna represented the antithesis of an ideal feminine self-identity for the girls, at least within the perimeters of the writing group where a norming effect dictated the girls' attitudes about attractiveness and dating violence.

During my encounters with the girls, I was privy to numerous stories about their dating relationships with boys. These stories often carried a mix of competing bravado for the audience of peers and tones of moral shame about their behavior evidenced by tagged-on phrases such as "I'm just playin'" to add ambiguity about the truth of various claims where physical intimacy or cheating were involved. To some extent these kinds of narratives were examples of the ways adolescent girls "play" with notions of female sexuality (Finders, 1997). Finders noted young adolescent girls try on various roles of female sexuality they see exhibited by women in the popular media, their social networks, and their families. Beyond the inherent nature of adolescent play, however, the narratives revolved around four key beliefs about dating: (1) girls must be physically attractive in order to be considered suitable for dating or "datable," (2) peers, boys, and the popular media regulate what is considered attractive physical attributes and behavior, (3) dating boys and being hurt by boys is an inevitable prospect for girls, and (4) girls are responsible for boys' behaviors towards them.

An analysis of what it takes to be physically attractive and thus "datable" dominated a great deal of the girls' talk with one another. Much of this belief was made evident in their group assessment of popular icons such as Rihanna. The peer influence of female attractiveness was not only publicly analyzed but also regulated through an attendant process of peer approval. Boys' opinions of their attractiveness carried a great deal of importance as well. For instance, in sixth grade, Samantha wrote in her journal, "A boy told me I was ugly. It was a good day until he said that." Similarly, a year later Tara wrote a narrative about a girl who developed an eating disorder because her boyfriend told her she was fat. After Tara read this piece to the group, other girls started talking about girls they knew who cut themselves with razors and other objects like the wire from their spiral notebooks. When I asked the group why this sort of self-injurious behavior happened, the girls responded unanimously that it always had to do with boys. Especially vulnerable to this behavior were girls in dating relationships where boys had a great deal of power over girls' sense of self-worth that was largely predicated upon their sense of fulfilling the behavioral and physical expectations of being a "datable" commodity.

Although dating was a new experience the girls were exploring in varying degrees through firsthand and secondhand accounts, all of the girls stepped unquestioningly into pre-formed beliefs about dating roles. They also regulated one another's behaviors and thus perpetuated rules for dating roles through their comments to one another about celebrities and peers. Dispensing advice about dating, in seventh grade, Felicia posted the following message on her *MySpace* page:

> When a Boy Wants a Kiss
> They hold your hand and always play with it.
> They stare into your eyes for a long time.
> They get close to your face.
>
> When a Girl Wants to Kiss You
> They stare into your eyes biting their lip.
> They always wrap their arms around you.
> They play with their hands, shirts, pants, etc.
> just waiting for you to make the move.

In this message, typical actions leading up to physical intimacy are described as a boy and a girl giving quiet signals to each other until the boy finally makes "the move." To be successful in engaging in physical intimacy with a boy, girls need to know how to play their part in this theatrical production.

During her eighth grade year, Tyshea wrote love poetry the entire time she participated in the group. As the following example illustrates, her poetry often carried an ominous tone about the inevitability of dating, heartbreak, and the challenging road of a long-term relationship.

In Time

In time I will get a little older and think I've found the right one

In time I will find out that he's not and get my heart broken

In time I will truly find the right one and get married

In time I will have my ups and downs

In time I will have children

In time I would have lived a whole life but till then all I can say is "In Time"

This kind of futuristic poetry writing with fatalistic undertones was common in the writing the girls produced. Imagined romantic relationships were often as fraught with as much emotional turmoil as real ones. Adrianna illustrated a sense of the inevitability of suffering in dating relationships in a poem she entitled "Love."

Love
There a time were you fall for the
one you love you reach into his
arms the day you start to cry. He
leans into your ear and say the
four letter word I love you girl to
the day that my life goes bye, you
say hes your baby the times go
through times get thick sometimes
thin but he is still your boo you
still sit back and think why he is
the one for me.

As she cast herself in a future role as the recipient of great love, Adrianna hinted at an attendant shadow of loss, of times that "get thick sometimes / thin." In this writing, Adrianna largely parroted a script she had internalized about dating from peers, the popular media, family, and other Discourse communities she was a member of where love for girls was equated to sacrifice. Much of the burden described in real or imagined relationships in such writing was largely placed on girls. Briana illustrated the hefty burden adolescent girls bear for relationships with boys in the following poem she crafted one day during the writing group.

MY POEM TO SOMEONE I LOVED AND I
RUINED IT!!!!!!!!

> I Never ever meant to make you cry but sometimes just you make my heart die
> when I think about you all the time I feel tears running down my cheek when I'm
> sitting underneath the peak.
> When you lose someone special you can't get it back until you see them with some-
> one else you say "see I could've been that girl getting whatever I wanted"

In this poem, Briana wrote about the anguish of regret she felt when she single-handedly "ruined" a relationship with a nineteen-year-old who had promised to marry her when she turned eighteen. Briana also depicted the status that accompanies being datable through being seen by others as the girl "getting whatever I wanted" from a boyfriend.

In all of these examples of writing, dating relationships with boys were given a dominant position in the girls' lives. The girls' ideas about their roles in romantic relationships carried an inherent value system that drew boundaries around their lives and determined their future happiness. A boy telling a girl she is ugly in passing at school was tantamount to being told she was not suitable for dating and thus would never fulfill her destiny as a female. By the same token, a girl's future as a girlfriend and wife was contingent upon her ability to successfully read a boy's cues for physical intimacy and if she did not pass this second test, after the first test of physical attractiveness, she constantly ran the risk that she would "ruin" the relationship altogether, which would lead to her blame over losing "someone special you can't get it back." Even a long-term relationship once obtained would be fraught with "ups and downs." With such rules and expectations for dating boys, is it any wonder adolescent girls slice into their skin to cope with the pressure they feel?

Harassment, Anger, and Fighting with Boys

In their writing, all relationships with boys carried an undercurrent of dating roles even when the girls wrote about "friends" or boys they encountered casually in school. These relationships were often problematic for the girls because of the perpetual instances of sexual harassment that went unchecked and became part of a generalized dating role they felt compelled to play irrespective of the social context. That is, the girls often operated within the norms of female dating behavior even when they were not participating or interested in dating various boys. Being in conflict over enacting the expected behaviors of dating with boys they were not romantically interested in often led to the girls expressing anger towards and even fighting with boys. One day a school police officer came to our group to follow up with Kecia on a report of a boy's inappropriate behavior with a girl in the school.

Officer: The counselor told me you'd be in here.

Simone: What'd the girl say again?

Officer: What happened?

Kecia: [In a serious tone of voice.] Ok. There was this girl sitting around me and I was sitting around this girl and I told on him. Now he tried to say that I lied and he yelled in my face and cussed and [inaudible].

Officer: Do I need to say something to him about that?

Kecia: About what?

Tia: I'll cuss him out.

Kecia: He was like—

Simone: Talk to him for you?

Kecia: [Indicates no to the police officer.]

Officer: Oh okay. It's your choice.

Kecia: He was like you lying you lying. I was like no cuz I actually saw your hand going up her skirt.

Tia: So did Coach A.

Kecia: I know Coach A did too.

Officer: What class is this?

Tia: Science.

Kecia: Well, it was in the hallway when we was uh. Oh! [Realizing the officer was shifting the topic to the present context of the writing group.]

In this exchange Kecia tried to sort through two offences of a boy putting his hands up a girl's skirt and attacking Kecia for reporting his behavior. The officer stayed focused on the cussing incident instead of the inappropriate touching. He was also quick to abandon the topic and move on to the context of the writing group although he lingered in the room for a while to joke around and even asked the girls if they had gone to church the previous Sunday for Easter as if to remind them of the necessity of a moral code. Opposite to the officer's approach, the girls clearly needed a venue for processing the incident. The girls also needed a space for learning about sexual harassment (Fine & McClelland, 2006). In this case, the authority figures in the school left the instance of sexual harassment for the girls to solve on their own with few tools other than after-the-fact fighting to try to stick up for one another, as in the manner of Tia's offering to "cuss out" the boy who had bullied Kecia. Alone, the girls knew less about how to keep one another safe from rude or offensive behavior by boys.

The girls characterized unwanted touching by boys at school both witnessed and experienced firsthand as a routine experience. A year after the incident involving the police officer, Kiara fumed with disgust in the writing group one day as she described ongoing incidents of getting humped on by boys while she stood in line for lunch in the cafeteria. When I asked her what the teachers and staff in the cafeteria did about it, she shook her head and explained with resignation, "They never see it happen." Towards the end of her eighth grade year Isabel told me "everything" her boyfriend did made her angry. When I asked for clarification, she explained the way he hit her arm playfully and touched her hair, every way he *touched* her made her angry.

Veronica captured the prevalence of male physical aggression towards girls through a power point she created about her day at school.

My Day
1st period tennis
I played tennis and ran around the courts.
We practice on our serves and talked about our tournament
Passing period
Walking when destiny tripped me cause I didn't talk to her.
2nd period science
We had a decision about the human body and how systems work.
Passing period
I was walking when Marcus hit me in the head and I chased him around.
3rd period choir
We learned the moves to our new song and started to sing.
Going to lunch
When going to lunch Destiny, Christy, and I were chasing Decorous cause he took Christy's binder.
Lunch
My friends got caught throwing food at Lorenzo and William.
Going to class
We had got in trouble by Mr. H. and he separated girls and boys.
4th period reading
Read some fluency pages and took some quizzes.
Passing period
Chris hit me with his papers.
5th period math

Played with some blocks and was looking for the areas.
Passing Period
I got hit by Chris again.
Passing Period
I got in trouble for hitting Chris and William.
6th period English
Read some books and poems.
7th period social studies
It was so fun we read some passages, then we watched a movie and talked.

In this text, Veronica described a typical day of perpetually being hassled by boys while also getting in trouble for retaliating against some of the boys. Her frustration and helplessness echoed Kecia's writing about the ways boys talked to her. In seventh grade, Alicia quickly generated the following list of names she had heard boys call girls when I asked the girls to write about words they did not like.

Boyz Names
Big lips
Bald head B***h
Donkey
Flat chest
Bald head chicken
Fat hog

Later in the same exercise I asked the girls to make a list of names girls call boys. Alicia wrote the following list:

Barry
Daniel
Marcus
Byron
Ty

Alicia's list of names boys call girls highlighted the way boys used language to both dehumanize girls and assault their physical appearance. On a different occasion in seventh grade, Kecia wrote another piece about the ways boys talk to her.

Boys

Different boys always talk about me when the talk about sometimes I shut up sometimes I talk back. They make me feel like I am nothing and it feel like I want to beat them up But I can't because I will get in trouble. I feel like I am nothing. I feel like I am nothing. Now I feel like I am something because if I wasn't pretty I won't get boyfriends.

In the first half of this writing Kecia lamented the fact that boys' comments made her feel like she is "nothing" and invoked feelings of both anger towards boys and helplessness within a school system that punished girls for boys' bad behaviors. Later in this writing, Kecia bolstered her confidence by noting she must be pretty because she is able to "get boyfriends." This writing also captured the conflict the girls felt over the ways boys' assessments of their appearances dictated their views of themselves. Being viewed as "pretty" by boys was equivalent to being datable and helped Kecia balance her feelings of being worthless. Whether physical or verbal in nature, the girls expressed a belief that they were virtuously powerless to change this culture of sexual harassment, and so they swallowed their anger as much as they could and slipped further into seeking relationships with boys who would be their protectors from the predatorial and demeaning behavior of other boys.

All-Girls Schools

In large-scale investigations into the benefits of single-sex public education, definitive gains in academic achievement have not been established (Institute of Education Sciences, 2005; Institute of Education Sciences, 2008). There has been a stronger favorable trend reported for socio-emotional factors such as fewer behavioral distractions in the classroom. According to a review conducted by the Institute of Education Sciences (2008),

> Teachers cited greater benefits of single-sex schooling for girls than for boys in 5 of the 10 benefits categories. That is teachers believed that girls benefit more than boys from better peer interactions, a greater emphasis on academic behaviors, a greater degree of order and control, socio-emotional benefits, and safe behavior. Teachers believed that both sexes benefit equally from single-sex education in terms of a greater sensitivity to sex differences in learning and maturation. (p. 27)

My experiences teaching in an all-girls' high school support the findings of this study. However, simply separating girls from boys in school does not teach girls and boys how to interact with one another in ways free from gender bias. Thus, as appealing as the idea of cloistering the girls in this study away entirely from boys in school became to me, I was not sure a school without boys would solve the deeply rooted issues of sexual harassment and gender identity based on narrow, heterosexual conceptions of dating roles the girls had to contend with. What I came to see clearly is the need for spaces in school curricula for girls to unpackage images and instances of male aggression towards females and expectations for dating roles in the girls' understandings of their interactions with boys. Such curricula could include an examination of the themes in books like White's (2002) *Fast Girls: Teenage Tribes and the Myth of the Slut*. Similarly, writing about these issues should not take place in the privacy of a hidden diary or words deleted as quickly as they are composed on a computer screen. In fact, like the need to address the instances of unchecked sexual harassment the girls experienced, it is important to encourage adolescent girls to write about their encounters with boys and understandings of gender roles. Such writing should not get lost in the hidden corners of girls' private writing. Rather, such writing should become the basis for critical inquiry (Lather, 1992). This kind of gender role examination should be part of a writing curriculum for at-risk adolescent girls. Instruction in writing, then, should include an examination of the gendered obstacles the girls encountered and had nowhere to go to address their anger. Kecia explained the emotional salve writing can provide, "when I write it down, I usually feel better about it." Thus, writing about painful experiences did help the girls sort through their feelings. As Frost (2001) recommended to classroom teachers, "the benefits of helping your students write about what is important to them" results in benefits such as "an element of control over some of the difficult—and often private—issues they may be facing" (p. xvii). Frost views this kind of writing as a way to release pent up emotions and regain psychological balance for adolescents.

Writing instruction for at-risk adolescent girls needs to go beyond emotional clearing to include systematic analysis of the topical patterns and themes recurring in their writing to engage in critical inquiry over issues like gender norms and sexual harassment. Without such examination over self-directed writing, girls such as the ones in this study will remain at risk of slipping further into false consciousness and academic alienation from school. For at-risk adolescent girls, the power code of writing must first be about dealing with gendered forms of oppression before contending with conventions of standard English. Such a power code moves beyond grammar and mechanics to include an understanding of the ways subjectivities are formed and power is proscribed to girls.

Concluding Vignette: "I Would Never Want to Go to a School without Boys"

Halfway through the second year in the project, Tyshea wrote one of the things she liked about school was boys. Curious about this statement, I told her that in past discussions in the group the girls had talked about the ways boys called them names and made fun of them. She thought about my comment briefly and responded, "Some boys are mean, but some boys I like" and smiled. Kecia and Alicia said they liked having boys at school too. Then, Kecia added she was mad at her boyfriend though because he called her a "B." Alicia added the word "witch" to make sure I got the full effect of the word without having to swear in front of me. I asked Kecia why he did that, and she explained he had asked her to the movies but she did not want to go, so he got mad and called her a bitch. Kecia barely made eye contact with me while she told this story with tones of both anger and defeat. I asked the girls what they would think about going to a school without boys. They all exclaimed shock and almost shouted "no way" to such a suggestion. "Why not?" I asked, shrugging my shoulders nonchalantly. The girls looked at me with an air of indignation and said they could not imagine what they would do at school without boys around. I told them I used to teach at an all-girls high school and that it was nice because the girls focused on learning. I explained, "Girls did not care about what they looked like and did not fight with one another. And, they all ended up going to really good colleges when they graduated. They went to school to learn." I could see the girls absorbing this idea slowly. They agreed that without boys around girls would not fight with one another but still could not conceive of a school without boys. A year and a half after this conversation, I asked Alicia again what she thought about going to a school without boys, to which she replied definitively, "I would never want to go to a school without boys."

References

Finders, M. (1997). *Just girls: Hidden literacies and life in junior high.* New York: Teachers College Press.

Fine, M. (1992). *Disruptive voices: The possibilities of feminist research.* Ann Arbor, MI: The University of Michigan Press.

Fine, M. (1988). Sexuality, schooling, and adolescent females: The missing discourse of desire. *Harvard Educational Review, 58* (1), 29–51.

Fine, M., & McClelland, S. (2006). Sexuality education and desire: Still missing after all these years. *Harvard Educational Review, 76* (3), 297–338.

Flake, S. (2005). *Who am I without him? Short stories about girls and the boys in their lives.* New York: NY: Hyperion Books.

Frost, H. (2001). *When I whisper, nobody listens: Helping young people write about difficult issues.* Portsmouth, NH: Heinemann.

Gee, J. (2005). *An introduction to discourse analysis theory and method.* New York: Routledge.

Institute of Education Sciences. (2005). *Single-sex versus coeducation schooling: A systematic review.* U.S. Department of Education, Washington, D.C.

Institute of Education Sciences. (2008). *Early implementation of public single-sex schools: Perceptions and characteristics.* U.S. Department of Education, Washington, D.C.

Lather, P. (1992). Critical frames in educational research: Feminist and post-structural perspectives. *Theory into Practice, 31* (2), 8–99.

Lewis, M. (1993). *Without a word: Teaching beyond women's silence.* New York: Routledge.

Pipher, M. (1994). *Reviving Ophelia: Saving the selves of adolescent girls.* New York: Ballentine.

Read, B. (2011). "Britney, Beyoncé, and me"—primary school girls' role models and constructions of the "popular girl." *Gender and Education, 23* (1), 1–13.

Sarroub, L. (2005). *All American Yemeni girls.* Philadelphia, PA: University of Pennsylvania Press.

Schultz, K. (2001). Constructing failure, narrating success: Rethinking the "problem" of teen pregnancy. *Teachers College Record, 103* (4), 582–607.

St. Pierre, E., & Pillow, W. (2000). *Working the ruins: Feminist poststructural theory and methods in education.* New York: Routledge.

Tolman, D. (1996). Adolescent girls' sexuality: Debunking the myth of the urban girl. In Bonnie J. Ross Leadbeater and Niobe Way (Eds.), *Urban girls: Resisting stereotypes, creating identities.* (pp. 255–271). New York, NY: New York University Press.

Weedon, C. (1994). *Feminist practice & poststructuralist theory.* Oxford, UK: Blackwell.

White, E. (2002). *Fast girls: Teenage tribes and the myth of the slut.* New York: NY: Berkley Books.

Chapter Five

"If a Girl Tell That Other Girl That They Not Afraid of Her That Turns into a Fight": Fighting for Power in and through Writing

Narrative Profile of Tara

Tara was an African American girl with long limbs, short hair, and a reputation for being the fiercest bully in the entire school. The C.I.S. campus coordinator referred to Tara as a "queen bee" and tried to help her learn to control her anger, which had a way of unexpectedly bursting forth in off-handed and bitter confrontations. In sixth grade, Tara hugged her favorite teachers, wore jeans every day, talked perpetually, attended church separately from her family on the "white side of town," and found herself in numerous physical fights with other students at the school. In the beginning of her participation in the writing group, instead of engaging in writing, Tara frequently stared at me with a sardonic smirk. When she did write, it typically consisted of a choked out, desolate sentence such as "I was looking at a black wall all day." Once in a while Tara would drop her constant chatter and sarcastic gaze to compose something longer than a sentence in her journal such as the following entry:

> Some days I fell like no one care about me because when me & my sister get in a fight she tell me nowone in my family like me & I know my anunt does not like me because she told me well she said "that why I don't like you to spend a night" that when I was six years old I have no clue why she dose not like me I love everabod in my family

Although Tara exhibited confusion and a degree of vulnerability in this writing, there was little that appeared to scare her. Tara was the only girl in the writing group who never expressed feeling intimidated by boys. In fact, in sixth and seventh grade Tara physically and verbally fought with boys over the smallest insult. Neither was Tara intimidated by girls. Periodically, other girls in the writing group spoke in awe of Tara's beating up eighth grade girls even though she was only in the sixth grade. No matter who her counterparts were in fights, Tara usually won. Tara also spent so many days during her sixth grade year sentenced to in-school suspension for aggressive outbursts that the writing group composed a collective poem in her honor about the pink slips teachers filled out to accompany her to the principal's office for disciplinary action.

Pink Slips
Hurting, Wounding, Frustrating
Pink Slips
Always
Give
Me a Headache

Through frequent verbal slights and mocking stares, Tara evoked more tears and arguments in the writing group than all of the other girls combined.

In seventh grade, Tara reappeared after the summer break taller, wearing braids in her hair, and talking about the numerous missionary activities she had participated in with her church's youth group. Tara declared she wanted to be a doctor when she grew up and wrote "Dr." on one side of her name card as a gesture of confidence about her future aspirations. In seventh grade, upon the advice of her mother, the Communities in Schools campus coordinator removed Tara from all C.I.S. projects, including the writing group, in the late fall due to her disruptive and back-talking behavior. Even so, Tara rarely missed an opportunity to poke her head into the C.I.S. classroom to say hello to me on the days the writing group met. Tara craved an audience and human contact but struggled with sincerity towards others. As a consequence, she toyed with female peers, boys, and authority figures she deemed to be unworthy of her respect. Of all the girls in the writing group, Tara sought my attention the most and yet hid huge portions of her life from me in a kind of dulled ambiguity that clouded over her words when too much clarity accidently slipped out. Tara never ceased to study me as much if not more than I studied her.

In eighth grade, Tara was permitted to return to the writing group, was elected president of the student body, and began to wear her hair in a small, side-swept ponytail adorned by a thin piece of ribbon tightly tied into a bow. In eighth grade with her reputation for fighting fully established, Tara ceased to engage in physical fights but did not cease to engage in subtle insults and deprecating remarks uttered with a mocking grin towards other girls in the group. Tara also demonstrated she could be a fierce advocate of students like Anna, who had Down's syndrome. As such, sometimes Tara donned the empathy of a protector defending more vulnerable others as she deemed appropriate. Other times, however, Tara was a caustic clown verbally slicing anyone in her path while staring defiantly and making a loud "tst" sound.

Little escaped Tara's notice and remark. Any feature, behavior, or word could become fodder for humiliating another student. For instance, Kecia wrote one day, "Today I am hurting because in 5th period Tara said I was going to be a crack head, then she said my babies is going to be deformed I got mad because the whole class was laughing at me I felt like crying." Even though, Kecia was part of the same clique of girls Tara hung out with, she rarely stood up to Tara. Tara was too bold and too relentless for most students to take any sort of consistent stand against. The years of fighting and intimidation tactics leading up to eighth grade had garnered Tara a great deal of power in the school. Whether students admired or despised her, they all respected Tara.

Tara sought power in other settings as well. In eighth grade, Tara had a boyfriend she "cheated on" at the mall. She wrote about this incident in the following narrative one April afternoon in the writing group.

The Affair

Okay it was a good day because I saw Lucas the other night. So me, Tia and Kecia. Went to the mall and Kecia boyfriend came and we saw this boy name zack and he was with a friend name Cody and wow he was smoking like HOT!!!!! So you know me I was missing around with him, just acting crazy... Then me him and Tia were about to go on the elevator but she walked of so it was just me and him then next thing I know we were kissing, and the bad part is that I have a boyfriend and like was acting

Through referring to the story for weeks afterward in discussions and in her writing, Tara appeared to draw a great deal of pleasure from this story and her friends' new label for her as a "player," which she quickly added to her cache of personal tropes that cast her in an omniscient role.

As a writer, Tara often volunteered to share her work but struggled with receiving feedback from other girls in the group. Tara's heightened awareness and manipulation of audiences in other venues made her keenly attuned to the risks of sharing writing with peers. When I asked Tara about her intended audience for her *MySpace* page, she answered her friends and the youth director from her church. Attending to an audience that contained her youth director made Tara feel she should minimize any hint of her troublemaker reputation on her *MySpace* page. Tara stated she designed her *MySpace* page to be "simple," free from "bad things," and intentionally misleading by claiming she was seventeen and lived in Los Angeles on her profile. Although she said she attempted to keep the images and words sanitized of anything that was too harsh, flashy, or non-Christian, she did post a comment that read, "Fake friends: will talk shit to the person who talks shit about you. Real Friends: Will knock them the fuck out." Such a post spoke to Tara's sense of justice and was reminiscent of the swift punishment for social infractions she often meted out in school.

As a behavioral phenomenon and motif in the girls' writing, fighting figured prominently into the weekly exchanges in the writing group. The C.I.S. campus coordinator viewed fighting as a broader "problem in the school" that played out occasionally in the writing group. While Tara's indirect aggression often served as a catalyst for confrontations in the group, no participant was immune to the influences of aggressive behavior inside or outside of the writing group. Indeed, fighting, like a partially healed wound vulnerable to tearing open with the lightest collision, continually fomented around the edges of whispers, pouts, and eyes suddenly welling with tears.

Research on Adolescent Girls' Aggressive Behavior

In the media, adolescents have long been depicted as children without a moral compass who fall prey to numerous socially concerning behaviors. Talk shows and movies such as *Kids* have portrayed adolescents as recklessly pressing towards adulterated behavior bordering on delinquency. In the past two decades, media portrayals of adolescent girls have increasingly been constructed in debase terms as well. Contemporary television shows like *Gossip Girl*, *Teen Mom*, and *The Secret Life of the American Teenager* have been constructed around fictional and real accounts of the sex lives of teenage girls. Movies such as *Heathers* and *Mean Girls* have also highlighted the Machiavellian nature of adolescent girls. Of this media trend, Winn (2011) noted,

> Many girls have been accused of departing from the heteronormative trope of "sugar and spice" to the reputation of "no longer nice." Everything from music videos, single mothers, and girls going wild has been placed on trial and found guilty for the disappearance of childhood and innocence for particular girls. (p. 4)

Similarly, popular books such as *Fast Girls* (White, 2002) that examined the archetype of the adolescent "slut" have underscored trends towards social deviancy in adolescent girls. Even though White argued the depiction of the adolescent slut who is sexually insatiable and "asks" to be used collectively by males is fundamentally a myth, her research still unearthed an atavistic, *Lord of the Flies* world where adolescents capriciously label a girl a slut and banish her from the "tribes" of other students in white, middle-class, suburban high schools. Through such popular culture depictions, girls have been increasingly taking center stage in media portrayals of things to fear about adolescents.

Even in the news media adolescents are often depicted as statistics representing numerous social concerns. In reference to such accounts, Brozo and Simpson (2007) contended most negative images of adolescents are greatly exaggerated and offered the following facts about adolescents' behavior to counter such pervasive views:

1. Youth and adults commit crimes at roughly equal rates.
2. The great majority of children 17 years and younger who are killed are killed by adults.
3. An increase in violent crime for youth and adults has been identical.
4. U.S. society as a whole has a violence problem. Senior citizens in the United States are more likely to kill someone than a European teenager.
5. Risks of murder and being victim to other crimes are extremely low in schools as compared to neighborhoods and homes.
6. Teenage birth rates are identical to those of the adults around them. Three-quarters of babies born to teenagers are fathered by adult men.
7. Teens rank third by age group in studies of when HIV infection was acquired. Nearly all HIV transmission to teens is from adults.
8. Suicide rates for high school age youths are half those of adults.
9. Teens are the least at-risk of drug abuse, whereas there have been record levels of middle-aged drug abuse.
10. Youths from homes where parents smoke or from social groups with high proportions of adults who smoke are three times more likely to smoke than others. (p. 5)

Brozo and Simpson's observations not only serve to abate prevailing notions that adolescents are social deviants but also raise compelling questions about the influence of adult behavior on adolescents. Namely, their list points out the ways adolescents have been scapegoated for mimicking behavior modeled by adults. The solitary gender-specific observation concerning who is typically fathering babies born to teenage girls directly illuminates the predatorial influence of adults on adolescents.

In tandem to the popular media portrayals of adolescent problems, a great deal of research has also been devoted to examining adolescents' maladjusted behavior. A growing body of this research in the past two decades has been concerned with the aggressive behavior of adolescent girls. Researchers in the field of social psychology have broken down girls' aggressive behavior into two categories: (1) direct aggression, which entails face-to-face confrontation and physical fighting, and (2) indirect aggression, also referred to as social aggression and relational aggression, which entails harming another through indirect means such as gossiping. Archer and Coyne (2005) identified the following behaviors as examples of indirect aggression exhibited by middle school students:

Gossip
Spread rumors
Backbite
Break confidences
Criticize clothes and personality behind back
Ignore
Deliberately leave others out of the group
Social ostracism/exclusion
Turn others against
Become friends with another as revenge
Imitate behind back
Embarrass in public
Anonymous notes
Practical jokes
Abusive phone calls
Dirty looks
Huddle
Roll eyes
Indirect physical aggression (e.g., vandalism) (p. 216)

Note that nearly all of these behaviors are contingent upon adept language skills. Thus, it stands to reason that individuals with the best verbal skills have the most leverage in perpetuating or countering indirect aggression.

While much of the early research involving female adolescent aggression argued feminine deviance accounted for such behavior, more recent research has identified female adolescent aggressive behavior as greatly shaped by gender identities (Cernkovich, Lanctot, & Giordano, 2008; Talbott, Celinska, Simpson, & Coe, 2002). For instance, Adams (1999) noted four prevailing theories as to why adolescent girls engage in aggressive behavior: (1) adolescent girls who fight present a "maladjustment to femininity" (p. 118), (2) adolescent girls who fight do so in "defiance of stereotypical feminine roles" (p. 118), (3) adolescent girls who fight are the product of "dysfunctional families and/or sexual abuse" (p. 119), and (4) adolescent girls who fight do so for ideological reasons such as poverty and competition for resources that necessitate resistance to dominant norms for female behavior. Contrary to these theories, Adams's research with middle school girls identified as "at-risk" for school failure because of their physically aggressive behavior highlighted the nuances of reasons adolescent girls fight, none of which fell solely into one of the aforementioned categories. Rather, Adams found two fundamental causes for adolescent girls' direct and physical aggression. In Adams's study, the primary reason adolescent girls fought with boys was to reclaim physical and psychological power in response to "the popping of bras, the grabbing of girls' behinds, and references to their breasts as 'hooters' and 'tits'" (p. 123). Adams also found adolescent girls fought with boys and girls alike to "prove their loyalty to a friend or boyfriend" in order to garner "a relational understanding of respect in which respect for others is paramount in maintaining solid, stable relationships" (p. 123). Adams referred to this latter category as "I'm not your friend" fights. In both of the rationales for fighting, Adams noted the girls' stories illustrated "the struggle adolescent girls have in constructing identities that defy erasure and dismissal" (p. 125). In other words, the adolescent girls in Adams's study fought to assert an empowered public identity.

With respect to identity formation, Crothers, Field, and Kolbert (2005) found a correlation between girls with a more traditional feminine gender identity and relational or indirect aggression entailing "a range of emotionally hurtful behaviors" that include things like gossip, social exclusion, and stealing friends (p. 349). Conversely, they found girls with a more masculine gender identity reported relying much less on relational aggressive behaviors and more on "emotional intensity and confrontation" (p. 353). Gender identity played a key role in the analysis of Crothers, Field, and Kolbert's study.

Talbott, Celinska, Simpson, and Coe (2002) found adolescent girls fight in response to social or indirect aggression, their interactions with boys, and to solidify group alliances. Of these categories, Talbott, Celinska, Simpson, and Coe highlighted the role of group alliances in adolescent girls' aggressive behavior. They noted, "Conflicts, disagreements, and fights are inexplicably linked to social group affiliations; they have implications for the social order of the group that extend beyond the boundaries of a given fight" (p. 205). Thus, Talbott, Celinska, Simpson, and Coe found fights both solidify and challenge group alliances.

In a report published by the U.S. Department of Justice, Lockwood (1997) found that instances of physical violence were "about the same" for adolescent girls as they were for adolescent boys (p. 3). Through an analysis of 250 incidents of violence reported by 110 middle and high school students, Lockwood noted certain "opening moves" led to an act of violence (p. 1). From an "opening move" such as teasing or offensive touching, adolescents made "a rational choice to be violent, a choice with generally one of three goals: to gain compliance, to restore justice, or to assert and defend identities" (p. 3). Thus, motives of retribution and saving face drove much of the adolescents' decisions to engage in physically aggressive fighting.

Echoing many of the findings from the above studies, the girls in the writing group cited three reasons why girls fight: (1) to confront negative gossip, rumors, or suspicions that friends have said bad things about them, (2) to confront negative situations with boys (e.g., stealing another girl's boyfriend, being displaced in a friendship by a boyfriend, fighting with boys who pick on them), and (3) to prove they are not afraid of someone else. Girls fought with boys and girls alike for these reasons. Of these categories, the girls placed blame on boys for the greatest number of fights occurring at school. For instance, Felicia said the fights she had with friends were more often than not predicated upon friends saying "you act different around boys and I'm like so do you and this causes arguments."

Most of the fights or threatened fights the girls reported occurred at school. Explaining this phenomenon, Simone, an eighth grade African American girl who spent one year attending the writing group, clarified the reason she engaged in fights in school,

> What I don't like in school is like I have to deal with somebody, you know, proba-
> bly wanting to fight me or something like that. Like I'm not scared of them, but I
> don't want to sit there and play with them.

With this commentary, Simone captured the necessity of fighting in school with a kind of resigned sadness. Simone had transferred to this school because she "didn't get along with the girls" at the school she had attended previously. Even at this new school Simone had a hard time developing friendships, explaining she had "associates" but not friends at the school. Simone was a large girl who felt she was often goaded into fighting because of her size. Even though she deplored fighting, she did not know how else to function in the face of the taunts and direct aggression she encountered in school.

Within the interactions of the girls in the writing group, I saw the girls' direct and indirect aggressive behavior come about as a way to establish a social caste system where slights often predicated upon ethnic and gendered stereotypes were used to try to insulate the girls from falling to the bottom rung of the social system in the school. Because of the girls' arguably low stature within the school, fighting had become a way to establish authority and as Simone noted a requirement of attending school. As such, whether the girls narrated stories of previous fights or engaged in them within the group, I came to see fighting as a way for the girls to push towards an identity of raced, classed, and gendered respect. Fighting allowed girls like Tara to (re)claim power and create their own mythologies, as it were, of legendary heroism.

Fighting within the Writing Group

During the second meeting of the writing group, I decided to engage the girls in an art activity as a springboard into writing. I passed around pieces of construction paper and asked each girl to select several pieces of paper. Then, I explained that one piece of paper would be their canvas or background and they were to tear the other pieces of paper into pictures and shapes to glue onto the background paper. I passed out glue sticks and watched the girls become quickly engrossed in their construction paper creations. After they finished assembling their pictures, I asked them to turn the paper over and write a title for their picture and three words, phrases, or sentences to describe it. Throughout this process, LaShonda, a sixth grade African American girl who had created a picture using the colors yellow, green, and red, held up her paper and asked me what she should call her picture. I said, "Your picture looks like a fiesta because of the bright colors and symmetrically patterned shapes." In response, LaShonda sweetly asked, "Are you Hispanic?" When I answered "no," she started making jokes about the title of her picture being about "meskins." I asked her what she had just said and through giggles, she repeated the word "meskins" and made some comments about "Hispanics" that I did not quite hear. To this, I stated, "Let's not use that language and say those things." LaShonda's giggling rose to a hysterical pitch. Then, she quipped between giggles, "Ok, I'll call it wetbacks." The intern who was present admonished LaShonda and told her the word "wetbacks" was just as bad. Trying to redirect LaShonda to the writing activity, I asked her what her picture was about, and still giggling she said it was the colors of the Mexican flag. One girl seated across the cluster of tables countered blandly, "No, you need white too for it to be the colors of the Mexican flag." LaShonda continued to giggle and, although she ceased to use racial epithets, she could not quite step away from her racist jokes about Latinos. At some point, I became aware of Samantha, a sixth grade Latina, sitting with her arms crossed and glaring at LaShonda on the other side of the gathering of tables and realized the depth of injury LaShonda's comments had caused her. After the writing group concluded for the day, Samantha quickly exited the room and did not return to the writing group for two weeks. This was my first glimpse into the ways indirect aggression served to establish social hierarchies such as ones based on ethnic divisions among the girls within the group and within the school at large. Such slights among the girls were common in the writing group but were usually dissipated after a few tense words. On one occasion, however, several of the girls got into a fight that required the guidance of three adults to sort out.

During the second year of the writing group, I asked the girls to think about what made each of them unique and then read to them the poem "By Myself" from *Honey, I Love and Other Love Poems* (Greenfield, 1978).

By Myself
When I'm by myself
And I close my eyes
I'm a twin
I'm a dimple in a chin
I'm a room full of toys
I'm a squeaky noise
I'm a gospel song
I'm a gong
I'm a leaf turning red
I'm a loaf of brown bread
I'm a whatever I want to be
An anything I care to be
And when I open my eyes
What I care to be
Is me

After reading the poem aloud and talking about it briefly, I asked the girls to trace their hands on a sheet of paper, hold up the pictures of their hands, and discuss what they noticed about one another's hands. As we went through this activity, I commented on the uniqueness of each of the girls' hands and how at the same time they were similar to one another. At one point in this process, Tara commented that Jenni's hand looked like a "girly-girl" hand because she had drawn pink nails and a ring on her hand. When I asked what "girly-girl" meant, Tara responded "prissy." To this, I asked, "What does 'prissy' mean?" Tara responded in a huff, "Tsst. You always askin' me questions." Ignoring Tara's tone, I repeated my question, "What does 'prissy' mean?" This time Kecia answered, "It means stuck up." Lexi added, "It's a bad word. It means conceited." So, I dug in a little and asked the rest of the group, "Is that what prissy means? To be stuck up or conceited?" Tara jumped into the conversation again and said, "No! It means you like to wear jewelry and do not like to climb trees and stuff like that." To this, my research assistant countered, "I don't know, I love to wear lots of jewelry, and I love to climb trees." Kecia reiterated her opinion, "Prissy means stuck up." To take the conversation to a deeper level of introspection, I asked the girls if they knew what a stereotype was. This question appeared to agitate Jenni, who began to become restless in her seat and cast mean looks at the girls on the opposite side of the room from her. I thought Jenni was embarrassed about the conversation surrounding Tara's opinion of her drawn hand, so I decided to move on to talking about writing a response to the activity. I was stopped from this plan, however, when I became aware that a couple of girls in the group were upset. I heard Kecia say in a negative tone, "I don't care if she don't like me." I could see she was upset, so I stopped talking and asked, "What's going on? What just happened?" The girls somewhat cautiously told me Jenni had whispered into Alicia's ear that she didn't like Kecia. Then, Alicia relayed the message to Kecia. Kecia then indignantly discussed the issue with Tia making statements that she did not care who liked and did not like her. With Kecia's voice becoming more audible, I became aware of the issue suddenly materializing in the group. The exchange had happened so quickly that I missed virtually all of it.

After the fact, I came to understand the fight was a long-time-coming fight built up from too many cafeteria whispers and dirty looks between Kecia and Jenni. Tara sparked the fight with a slight towards Jenni by saying the picture of the hand she had drawn looked "prissy." On the heels of this comment, Alicia whispered to Jenni "do you like her" [referring to Kecia]. Once Jenni's response of "no" was passed around the circle to Kecia, Tia fanned the flames through indignant sighs and slamming her hands on the table abruptly dissolving my plans for writing.

Alicia, Tia, Kecia, and Tara were all seventh grade African American girls and members of the same clique. Jenni, a sixth grade Latina girl, without a similar cohort in the room to take her side, bravely stood her ground alone. I tried futilely to resolve the fight by asking Kecia and Jenni to talk about why they were mad at each other. Jenni revealed Kecia was always making fun of her in the cafeteria with other older girls. Kecia only shrugged, rolled her eyes, and glared. So, I asked both of the girls to write about their feelings. Kecia refused but Jenni wrote, "b/cuz the furst day of CIS she would roll her eyes at me and when I have a comment she always gets all mad at me and rolls her eyes." Jenni read her writing out loud, which served to incite the anger among Kecia's clique of friends further. Tia stormed out of the room and reappeared a few minutes later still muttering indignant complaints towards Jenni. Tara made rude comments about my efforts to engage in conflict resolution between Jenni and Kecia, so the C.I.S. campus coordinator took Tara out in the hall to talk to her about her behavior. When Jenni got up to leave the writing group, Tia and Kecia jumped up to follow her. My research assistant trailed all of the girls outside and stood guard at the school entrance until Jenni's mother drove up to retrieve her.

After this fight, Kecia disappeared from the writing group for several weeks and did not reappear again until nearly the end of the school year. Jenni came back one more time for the Christmas party, but even then she mistrustfully glared around the room at the witnesses to the fight and then never returned to the writing group. Although I talked to both girls repeatedly about returning to the writing group, the layers of hurt with this fight were too many for Jenni to traverse. Jenni's absence and Kecia's clique, however, eventually pulled Kecia into attending the group again.

Fighting in School

During the second year of the study, I asked the girls to draw a map of the school and put dots where they had seen a fight occur over the past year. After having the girls hold up their maps so we could all get a collective sense of the number of dots, the girls began telling stories of aggression that accompanied the dots on their maps. As I listened to their conversation, I jotted down the following traces of narratives about fighting:

> "It makes me want to whop them" (Tara).
> "Even my mom hits me" (Briana).
> "One of them kids called me a wolf baby" (Alicia).
> "He called me a he/she" (Kecia).
> "I remember when I fought this girl in the bathroom" (Tara).
> "When Tara was in sixth grade, she fought an eighth grader" (Alicia).
> "I've never seen Kecia fight" (Briana).
> "Oh man, and I have to go to church today" (Tara).
> "It's funny when girls fight" (Alicia).

Throughout this discussion, the girls talked about violence in a matter-of-fact manner and almost bored tone of voice. Fights were merely part of the landscape of their lives. Briana's map, like the other girls' maps, depicted the location of fights as being fairly equally distributed around the building, occurring everywhere except in classrooms.

Briana's Map of Fights at School

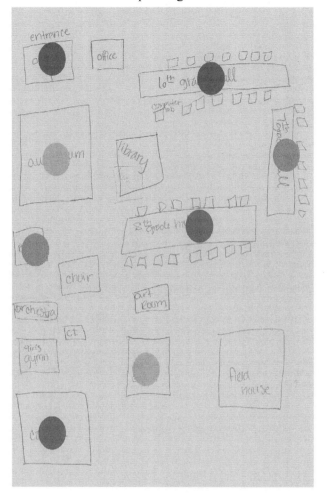

In tallying up the places the girls identified fights occurring over the past year in the school from this activity, I came up with the following breakdown of the locations in the school where the girls had witnessed at least one physical fight:

Sixth grade hall	12
Eighth grade hall	10
Seventh grade hall	9
Auditorium	6
Cafeteria	5
Entrance to the school	5
Main office	4

Band room	3
Gym	3
Boy's Bathroom	2
Girl's Bathroom	1
Choir Room	1

From this snapshot, the hallways, where there was lots of movement, physical proximity, and little adult supervision, were the most volatile areas of the school.

Around the time of the map activity in the writing group, Alicia wrote the following narrative about the behind-the-scenes retorts and opening moves that led to a fight at school.

> It was me and this girl Alexandra we were best frinds until she had to jump in to it and started calling me all these names and I sayed sticks and stones may Bake my Bones but words will never hurt me and she told me to shut up and I shut does not go up gas prices do and so later that day we were going to 6th period and she bumped itto me and I told her next time to say excise me and she said 'no' and she came back and punched me and I punched her back and we started fighting and we both got sent to the office and we had I.S.S. for the rest of the week.

Alicia's story captured the ways anger can suddenly escalate between the shifting tides of friendship in middle school and lead into a physical fight.

A year after the map activity, Felicia wrote the following piece about a colossal fight that was planned between two groups of girls one afternoon in the writing group when she was in sixth grade.

> The Big fight!!
> Well there is going to be some girls fighting!!!!
>
> When: 6:00-7:00
> Where: At the Park
> Why: Some reason
>
> And the stupidest thing is I'm going to be there.
> The thing is I'm not going to fight.
> Well I am running out of words.
> Sincerely,
> Felicia Vallez

When I asked Felicia why the girls were going to fight, she said she did not know. The social significance of the fight, however, superseded her need for a historical reason. Fortunately, the following week Felicia told me the school's police found out about the planned fight and showed up at the park to thwart the brawl. Instead of fighting, the girls fled the park.

Writing about Anger and Fighting beyond School

Narratives of anger were sprinkled throughout the girls' writing in connection with fighting. Fighting tied to anger was often depicted in courageous and justice-seeking terms as a way to reclaim power that had been usurped from the girls. Fighting was a way to right social wrongs. In the following piece, which I referenced briefly in the introductory chapter, Amber struggled to come to terms with her unusual feelings of happiness and how she could cope with the inevitable experience of someone making her angry. For Amber, "feeling krunk" was a heightened state of mind, which while helping her feel happy could also lead her into a "ghetto" fight. In this writing, Amber depicted fighting as a way to demonstrate psychological dexterity and power. Moreover, Amber viewed the way one handled anger through being in control of fighting as a facet of one's self-esteem.

Feeling Krunk
Today I woke up and I just felt krunk. Man I haven't
never felt like this man I think I'm scaring my self
With this crap. But if someone gets my nerves
I might go ghetto in that time. But who knows
I might Just calm down. But all people think
I'm a ghetto girl from the hood, but I know I'm
not just that I'm more than that. I'm a smart,
strong minded girl with goals and future. I
know this might be what some people say and
it never happens. Because they might get all
strung out but I know that isn't going to me,
but that because I seen it happen so much in
my family. Know that I'm krunk I would be in
someone's face in a second but I'm trying to
just calm down so I have to listen to my krunk
music. A little bit of plies. Some Lil Wayne,
Audio Push an a lot more. But know I think
I am not so krunk after listen to my music.
SO WHAT DO YOU DO WHEN YOU KRUNK?

In this narrative, Amber described being krunk as an agile state of mind in which she was empowered to choose to fight or ignore things that might upset her. For Amber feeling krunk was a positive emotion linked to feeling in control of a fight. In a mental state of "feeling krunk," Amber was in command of the opening moves that could lead to a fight.

In the girls' narratives of anger, fighting was an implicit threat that perennially lurked around the backdrop of a story. For instance, Kiara wrote about her accumulating anger towards a chronic family problem she was growing weary of.

!32!
You may ask why my title is 32... It's because 32 is how much money my step dad brought home as his pay check. Now this, this is a problem with mom. It's crazy because while mom spends a lot of time working her ass off trying to get all the bills taken care of, Danny does nothing all day long. All he really does is say that he is working but when we came home he was drunk. We told him if he could clean the house at least. And once again we get there and he is lying down drunk and the house looks like shit!!!☹ But no matter what we do to try and make him learn that it is bad for him, but he still drinks and does whatever and its soooooooo annoying.

In this narrative, Kiara blended her adolescent perspective with her mother's adult persona using the plural pronoun "we." With this rhetorical move, Kiara positioned herself as a powerful ally in the ongoing fight between her mother and her stepfather. Although Kiara's anger was a brewing caldron of anger towards a situation she felt powerless to change, by taking on the stance of another adult in the family admonishing her stepfather for wasting money on alcohol needed to pay household bills, getting drunk, and not helping around the house, Kiara constructed a more empowered subjectivity for herself. In effect, her anger moved her into an imagined fighting stance towards her stepfather.

Felicia adopted a similar stance in a narrative she wrote about her father and the anger he invoked in her.

Why does he have to be my father?
You no it kind of sucks how my dad is and I wish he was different. It really hurts me how I see other girls with there dad. And I never had a dad there for me. He was just too busy taking care of SOME OTHER KIDS who *ARENT EVEN HIS!* You no what that stupid lady Rachael had cursed at us and called us so many bad words and my dad don't do nothing. That's cuz he lives but not even 5 blocks away!! He doesn't even TRY to come and see us he just makes excuses! O.M.G you won't even believe this when we were little he would say I will go pick you up so yawl get yawls clothes ready so we would and be waiting on the porch and he would never show up! YOU don't know how much that hurt me! For my own dad to lie to us like that and get us all excited! IM really glad that my mom is there for me cuz without her I think I will so crazy! She is the one who supported me through all my pain. I think that's why I wont ever except any other guy she is been with I cant even except my step dad knowing he has been with me for 4 years!! Well you no sometimes I get in trouble for not respecting him or my dad, but tell me this if someone doesn't respect you then why should you respect them. I sure in heck no that my DAD don't respect me. My step thinks he does but if I did what he did too me than NO WAY!!

I would say that he and my dad is a punk because they don't know how to take care of there own kids!

In Felicia's narrative of the anger she felt towards her father and her stepfather, she implored the reader to see her perspective, to empathize with her feelings. Felicia also implied her anger towards her father was more than likely eventually going to be resolved through fighting. In other words, the day she expressed her anger towards these men would be the day she finally found the courage to fight them.

Trying to make sense of the anger and fighting she had observed, Veronica wrote the following poem in an attempt to take control of anger.

> *~who you are~*
> Who you are is who you are and that's never going to change.
> So why cant people stop judging us because were all the same.
> We all might be different colors in or out,
> But that's the way god has us,
> No matter what there's no doubt.
> We can act different no common interest it's okay.
> That's what makes us special in each individual way.
> Aren't you tired of this world full of pain?
> Why can't we all be different but yet the we all the same.
> We will yet all struggle and have all these fights,
> But some how, some way we will all reunite,
> Why can't we have a nation where there are no more fights?
> No more anger, no more pain, just a world with fun each day.
> Who we are is who we are and that our special way.
> Who we are is who we are were all different but it is okay

All of these examples of writing demonstrate instances of the girls' giving voice to different scenarios of oppression that cause anger and fighting. Through their writing about anger, the girls could talk back to their oppressors and shift their stance from one of victim to one of heroine. Writing about anger allowed the girls a place to imagine and rehearse a new persona for themselves. Such writing allowed the girls to "feel krunk," cuss out their stepfather, and cope with the worry in their lives. Through writing about anger, the girls were in a position to analyze their experiences and move towards reconciliation in their understanding of fairness. Writing not only gave the girls a place to vent their frustrations, but it also helped them to imagine being powerful and think through ways to confront anger. Writing was a means through which to cope with injustice to help prevent an escalation of aggression and fighting. Writing offered the girls a path out of the anger they felt and a way to imagine a different conclusion to the oppression they experienced.

Fighting, Anger, and Critical Literacy

Because fighting in many respects was endemic to the culture of the school and a way of life for the girls, writing about fighting presented an important point of entry to enacting a philosophy of critical literacy. Writing about anger and fighting offered the girls a place to mine emotions, reconsider aggressive behavioral patterns, and understand anger through reflective mechanisms. Instances of aggression, the opening moves to fighting, and histories of retaliation were all opportunities for the girls to examine the inequitable social structures such as group allegiances and gender roles that were the subtexts of fights. Lankshear and McLaren (1993) described critical literacy essentially as an examination of inequitable distribution of power. They explained:

> In short, literacies are ideological. They reflect the differential structured power available to human agents through which to secure the promotion and serving of their interests, including the power to shape literacy in ways consonant with those interests. Consequently, the conceptions people have of what literacy involves, of what *counts* as being literate, what they see as "real" or "appropriate" uses of reading and writing skills, and the way people actually read and write in the course of their daily lives—these all reflect and promote values, beliefs, assumptions, and practices which shape the way life is lived within a given social milieu and, in turn, influence which interests are promoted or undermined as a result of how life is lived there. Thus literacies are indices of dynamics of power. (p. xviii)

To move the philosophical orientation of critical literacy into practice, Van Sluys, Lewison, and Flint (2006) created the following typology to both implement and evaluate enactment of critical literacy:

1. disrupt the commonplace
2. consider multiple view points
3. focus on the sociopolitical
4. take action

This typology is a powerful heuristic for moving adolescent girls towards greater clarity about their anger and liberation from instances of oppression. As such, a pedagogy predicated upon a philosophy of critical literacy could be key in altering the culture of fighting in many schools. Before we enact any more sweeping reform bills predicated upon insuring basic academic proficiencies like the 2001 No Child Left Behind legislation, we need to attend to the cultures of fighting taking place in schools. In essence, how can students master basic proficiency in literacy without mastering basic proficiency over the causes of aggression towards peers?

Concluding Vignette: Still Fighting

One of the last pieces of writing Tara composed in the writing group was about trying to control her impulse to go along with what she deemed to be "wicked" peer behavior.

Psalms 39:1

And I say I will watch my way and keep my tongue from sin; I will put a muzzle over my mouth as long as the wicked is in my presence.

I really like this verse because when I get around my friend it seem like I want to for get every thing and go along what ever one else is doing and saying and do and for get the fact that I am a Christian. Which it should not be that way because it's like I am denying god and the bible says "deny me on earth and I will deny you and hea- ven". Then ever Sunday and Monday I go to church and every one sees me as such a faith full girl, so this weekend I went to this thing called sage for teen Christian girls and the lord really spoke to me and so over the weekend I layed ever thing down to the lord, ever since I did that I have been missing a lot of opportunities that I been missing because I been trying to hang out with the wrong crowed.

This piece demonstrated Tara's growth as a writer over the three years she participated in the group. Tara had evolved from her initial writing that consisted of brief glimpses like "Mrs. Mellinee sweet to me give me hugs when I'm in need" to a webbed introspection about the connections between her actions and her moral ideals. In "Psalms 39:1," Tara described a battle she was waging with herself and her sense of Christian ethics. Tara articulated the perimeters of the fight but did not declare a clear winner.

Two years after Tara wrote "Psalms 39:1," when she was a sophomore in high school, I ran into the youth director at her church and immediately inquired about Tara. The youth director said she had decided to remove Tara from further participation in the youth group because of the amount of discord she was causing in the group through indirect aggression. Tara was fighting with one of the other girls in the group and through this fighting had split the entire youth group into two teams in favor of and in opposition to Tara. The youth director was planning to counsel Tara individually but felt forced to remove Tara in favor of restoring peace to the group. She did not know what else to do. I felt saddened by the thought of the conversations that had taken place with Tara telling her she was once again being removed from a group. I had hoped Tara would outgrow such behaviors but after the years of being a bully in middle school, Tara was still fighting for power. Tara was still struggling to work out a sense of justice.

References

Adams, N. (1999). Fighting to be somebody: Resisting erasure and the discursive practices of female adolescent fighting. *Educational Studies, 30* (2), 115–139.

Archer, J., & Coyne, S. (2005). An integrated review of indirect, relational, and social aggression. *Personality and Social Psychology Review, 9* (3), 212–230.

Brozo, W., & Simpson, M. (2007). *Content literacy for today's adolescents: Honoring diversity and building competence,* 5th ed. Upper Saddle River, NJ: Pearson.

Cernkovich, S., Lanctot, N., & Giordano, P. (2008). Predicting adolescent and adult antisocial behavior among adjudicated delinquent females. *Crime & Delinquency, 54* (1), 3–33.

Crothers, L., Field, J., & Kolbert, J. (2005). Navigating power, control, and being nice: Aggression in adolescent girls' friendships. *Journal of Counseling & Development, 83,* 349–354.

Greenfield, E. (1978). *Honey, I love and other love poems.* New York, NY: Thomas Y. Crowell Company.

Lankshear, C., & McLaren, P. (1993). *Critical literacy: Politics, praxis, and the postmodern.* Albany, NY: State University of New York Press.

Lockwood, D. (1997). *Violence among middle school and high school students: Analysis and implications for prevention.* Washington, DC: National Institute of Justice Research in Brief, Department of Justice.

Talbott, E., Celinska, D., Simpson, J., & Coe, M. (2002). "Somebody else making somebody else fight": Aggression and the social context among urban adolescent girls. *Exceptionality, 10* (3), 203–220.

Van Sluys, K., Lewison, M., & Flint, A. (2006). Researching critical literacy: A critical study of analysis of classroom discourse. *Journal of Literacy Research, 38* (2), 197–233.

White, E. (2002). *Fast girls: Teenage tribes and the myth of the slut.* New York, NY: Berkley Books.

Winn, M. (2011). *Girl time: Literacy, justice, and the school-to-prison pipeline.* New York, NY: Teachers College Press.

Chapter Six

"My Mom Sometimes She Could Be Like Cool": Seeking Common Ground in the Labyrinth of Writing To, For, and About Mothers

Narrative Profile of Felicia

Felicia was a petite Latina girl with a sculpted face, dark shinning hair, and two symmetrical dimples that became visible whenever a wide grin emerged on her face. As a new member to the writing group during her sixth grade year, Felicia approached composing with a great deal of immediacy, sincerity, and focus. Felicia was comfortable with sitting down to a blank screen or blank sheet of paper and conjuring text out of thin air. Felicia rarely spent time searching for topics to write about and was extremely industrious in her approach to composing. Sometimes her writing was a carnivalesque romp through multimodal text; sometimes her writing was sobering; sometimes her writing was both. Like other girls in the group, Felicia leaned on writing to pull herself through difficult times in her life. As such, Felicia's writing was often intensely personal and deeply intertwined with the daily events of her life.

Felicia called a journal she wrote in at home her "BFF" (best friend forever), explaining, "Sometimes if I can't sleep or if something happens in the night, I'll get up in the morning and write about it." Tucked into a heating vent in her room, Felicia methodically hid her journal from her mother in order to keep her writing secret. When I asked Felicia about what compelled her to write in her "BFF" journal she stated, "Because some kids can't tell other people. They can just tell paper. Instead of putting the drama out there, you can just put it on a piece of paper." Felicia wrote in her journal about things that weighed on her mind throughout the day like her younger brothers getting spanked before school. Felicia's journal gave her a place to testify to such events as if documenting them would increase her power in a situation she felt otherwise helpless to change. In this manner, journal writing was Felicia's solace, reprieve, and source of empowerment.

In seventh grade, Felicia became best friends with Kiara, ended her friendship with Isabel, and began dating a boy she saw primarily at school. She also began to approach writing with increasing amounts of gravity in the group. Through the three years I worked with Felicia, her goals for herself as a writer remained largely focused on the idea of one day writing a book. At the end of her seventh grade year, Felicia stated she would like to write a book about herself "to have in my room or something and every day add something in my book and like chill when I'm older." As Felicia reflected over what would comprise the contents of a book about her life, she added, "So like sometimes it's funny or something and you can go back in your writing and think of it again and just like laugh or something." When I asked Felicia about other goals for herself as a writer she stated,

> I think if I was older, I think I would be a better writer because I would know more words and stuff. But if I do have a chance and if I really want to be I would be a writer that writes in books and stuff like publishing. I would like to probably make a book or two. Cuz, you could write a whole book about certain days—just making sense.

Felicia saw value in writing about her life, especially certain days in her life. In fact, Felicia often viewed events in her life through the lens of writing as if writing about such events added significance and a sense of permanence to them. Felicia also liked to write in her journal by hand because, as she stated, "Handwriting just like makes me calm down sometimes."

In the writing group, Felicia preferred to write in a multimodal format. She often composed on power point slides, incorporated animation and sound into her writing, and included clip art or photographs downloaded from the Internet. In terms of generating topics for writing in the group, Felicia used criteria predicated upon a narrative structure to select her ideas. Felicia explained, "I just like think about whatever pops into my mind. I create categories in my mind. I look at which one [idea] has the most story to it, the most problems in it and then I pick that one and just start writing about it."

Divining an audience for her writing was the most challenging aspect of composing for Felicia. Primarily, Felicia wrote for a fairly restricted audience to maintain her privacy. Felicia explained, "I don't know. I just like always send it to my aunt Candi. I don't really talk to her about boys. My aunt Candi if it's like real bad then she will tell my mom." After considering for a moment, Felicia added, "I mostly think about myself [as an audience]." Writing for a particular audience also shaped Felicia's topics. Felicia elaborated,

Sometimes thinking, thinking what to write about that's hard for me. Like at school I don't really want to write about home stuff because I don't know who told but one time I told a teacher stuff and then I told my Mom I told her and then my mom said she could have, I don't blame her because that's the rules that you have to call C.P.S. [Child Protective Services]. We were involved with that [Child Protective Services]. Then, I got in trouble because I told her. I don't want to tell like make it I don't want to like tell everything at school what happened my whole life and stuff because I know some of it's bad, and I don't want it end up carrying out there to where they'd be involved with C.P.S.

After telling this embedded narrative, Felicia summarized the role of an audience such as a teacher in composing, "I got to know like is this too personal for me to write or not." Felicia's barometer for writing being too personal for a particular audience also included her mother.

In an interview at the end of her seventh grade year, Felicia described a complicated relationship with her mother and her wish to be "close" with her mother. Felicia rarely wrote about her mother in the writing group. The first time she wrote about her mother was in a piece she composed quickly and saved to my jump drive without my having a chance to read it during the group. When I discovered the piece later, I felt numb as I absorbed the reality of this young adolescent girl's life with so many dreams of becoming a writer.

On Saturday

Well it on started when I wanted to go to the movies! I had to go to the movies but with a friend. So I invited Kiara! So we went to the movies, watched bride wars and had fun. Anyways we went home played a lot for a while. Then I started feeling sick! So then the night lasted for along tie-On did I tell you my mom went out to the club with my step-dad. they got home an they had drank to much! So they invited 2 of Donny's (step dad)sisters. Well 1 of Donny's sisters had a boyfriend and his brother was there to. My mom told them she had to go to work so if they could leave. well they did so it was my mom, me, kiara, and my 3 brothers. Well here were it began. That night @ 2:00 at night a man came into the house and tried to rape my mom she came running into the room! She was saying get away from but he didn't!

The following week, I discussed the piece with Felicia and the incident of the intruder. She told me, "Miss, I was scared!" but also stated her mom was ok. It turns out the man who broke into their apartment was a neighbor who later declared to Felicia's stepdad, "I'll rape whoever I want." Even though Felicia's stepdad confronted the neighbor, police charges were never filed.

At the end of seventh grade, Felicia won an award for having a high test score on a state mandated standardized math test, her boyfriend broke up with her because he said she got "mad too fast," she was selected to work as a student assistant for a summer camp at the school, and her mother made her get rid of her *MySpace* account because she did not feel the content was appropriate. In eighth grade, Felicia stopped being best friends with Kiara, continued to write in her journal, and began dating a new boy. Towards the end of eighth grade, Felicia wrote the following piece about introducing her new boyfriend to her family and meeting her boyfriend's mother. Bringing such introductions into her relationship with a boyfriend she interacted with primarily at school carried a great deal of significance for Felicia.

He's Great

Okay well if you're wondering why my title is different from this writing it's because his favorite color is dark green and mine is lime-green! Men and its just so crazy cuz we have so much in common. I like him a lot!! You no it feels like he's the best guy anybody can ever have. He is sweet, nice, dependable, trustworthy and loyal! Oh and the most important thing I forgot to say is his name is GIOVANNI! Heyy um um yesterday he played at the park with my brothers EVEN MY BIG BROTHER. It kina felt acquired but idk! And I am actually trying to let him and my Madre meet! I talk about him a lot to her and I think she's like ooooohhhwwwww Fela really like him! And by the way FELA is my nick name! ha-ha and he calls me that too and says it funny! So by all this stuff I am telling you. You think I should stay with him? ☺ I think I should!!

Oh and like   he is so romantic!! Oh oh oh and you no wat shocked me is HE ASKED IF I WANTED TO MEET HIS MOM and NOBOBY AT ALL HAS EVER ASKED ME THAT! I think that wat is so important!!

The approval of her mother and her boyfriend's mother elevated the importance and sense of permanence of this relationship for Felicia. A few weeks later, Felicia wrote another piece about the significance of meeting her boyfriend's mother.

♥NeRv0uSnEsS♥

Hey well today I am nervous because I am supposed to meet Giovanni's Mom. She sounds kool its just he is the first boy who ever ask to meet his mom! And he ready met my mom on Friday cuz she picked him up from the banquet and took him to our HOUSE!!! It was kind of acquired but it was fun! We took pictures and they came out so cute!! So I think his mom wants a copy! Well that's watt he was telling me but men I am so freaking nervous to meet her! I like her how it sounds when she is on the phone! And she even kinda reminds me of my mom! I just hope I don't have butterflies in my stomach when I do meet her!! I really hope she likes me! Do you think she will???

In eighth grade, Felicia wrote longer texts, drifted apart from her clique of friends, and became more outspoken about issues she faced with her parents. Offering a glimpse into her home life Felicia stated,

> Because it's like I don't know I just to me like my parents are like always always arguing and I know that when you go with CPS [Child Protective Services] they say that your parents are supposed to take classes and stuff but to me and sometimes it feels like we never should have went because it's still the same they just don't argue like worser. They still argue but it makes me really mad because she tells him like the meanest stuff and then like all of a sudden they're like better the next day and then I'm like should I be nice to him or not? And when I decide to be mad at him she's still with him. She like gets with him so I'm like why'd I do that or something? Or, sometimes she takes his side a lot and she takes our side too but sometimes it's just like—this is exactly like how I feel like when she's mad at him she pays more attention to us and she gives us a lot of attention but then when she gets back with him it's like the attention is on him and so I'm like. I tell my brothers that I don't really want to tell them because I don't want them to like tell my mom.

Both Felicia's stepdad and her biological father were a source of anger and disappointment to her. Felicia's mom was a conundrum to her. Her mother was a friend who put highlights in her hair, did her nails, waxed her eyebrows, teased her mildly about boyfriends, and yet remained unpredictable in her loyalties. Weighing all of these realities, Felicia summarized her relationship with her mother, "My mom sometimes she could be like cool but then when she's in her moods I don't have a good relationship with her."

The Mother-Daughter Continuum

In the past three decades, feminist scholars have written a great deal about the blurry interpersonal boundary between being a daughter and being a mother (e.g., Hirsch, 1981; Rich, 1976). Kerpelman, Shoffner, and Ross-Griffin (2002) described this phenomenon from the perspective of expectations. They wrote, "Much of what a daughter expects for herself comes from perceiving what her mother expects of her" (p. 290). Similarly, Hirsch (1981) noted mothers and daughters exist in a reflexive relationship that embodies "a discourse of plurality" (p. 211). Hirsch argued much of this reflexive and pluralistic relationship is due to the fact that daughters and mothers imagine their lives on a mutual timeline that extends across their generations of being a daughter and being a mother. Another variable often noted in the body of feminist research on mother-daughter relationships is the challenge of living in a social context where mothers and daughters must swim separately and together within a shared tide of sexism.

Although the girls' depictions of their relationships with their mothers were not a major motif in the girls' writing, because of the significance of mothers in research on adolescent girls' socialization (e.g., Thomas & King, 2011) I found the implications of such references to bear significance in their development as writers. Virtually all of the girls in the writing group reported wishing they had a close relationship with their mothers even though nearly all of them also reported keeping secrets from their mothers as they moved between the world of their peers and the expectations of their mothers. Felicia's relationship bore the extra strain of uncertainty about her mother's shifting stance towards her. From my distant, daughter-focused perspective, the reflexive and pluralistic nature of the mother-daughter relationship the girls reported consisted of a constant negotiation of trust, mistrust, interdependence, independence, attention, and disregard. In fact, one of the great riddles that emerged in this project was the ways the girls depicted their relationships with their mothers. Mothers were simultaneously confidants and clueless to the girls' behaviors, listened to and ignored, revered and despised. This multitude of stances towards their mothers was cultivated by a kind of psychological drift from peers' ideations, media images, the social milieu of the school that dominated their lives, and the roles their mothers adopted towards them. All of these influences not only served to advance a process of adolescent identity formation through separation individuation (Meeus, Iedema, Maassen, & Engels, 2005) but also made it necessary for the girls to cultivate a space where they could coexist with their mothers. In this process of seeking common ground, the girls depicted their mothers as being both quasi-peers and strict authoritarians; present and absent; devoted to their daughters and minimally aware of their daughters' lives. Illustrating this schism, Felicia had posted two comments side by side on her *MySpace* page that read, "A mother's treasure is her daughter," and "If you think I'm a BITCH, you should meet my MOM."

With respect to writing, the girls mostly hid their writing from their mothers out of fear of the reaction their writing would elicit. For instance, when Simone was in eighth grade, her mother admonished her for writing the following poem about boys when she could have written about God.

FFDD LALA CICI

Dang these boys be fine this go with my rhyme but some just aint worth my time
Dang why they gotta be so fine!!
I see my mamas point of view which just aint cool. But I am done chasing u. Cuz my mama from the hood and dats good.
I hope u got money and u aint broke and u even though that's not what im dating u for.
CUZ ima a DIVA

When I asked Simone about her relationship with her mother she stated, "We're close. Yes, she knows everything [about me]. She finds out one way or another." In another example, Samantha demanded the girls in the group tear her poem about her boyfriend from the book of writing we had created just in case her mother saw it. As both of these examples demonstrate, keeping writing from their mothers, often a goal the girls expressed in the group, required vigilance.

When the girls wrote about their mothers it was often from a stance of protection, guilt, and degrees of adoration. Tia revealed a glimpse into this bramble of emotions toward her mother when she was in sixth grade in the following writing.

Why I want to wish a you happy birthday

I want to wish you a happy birthday a happy because I love you for keeping me nice and warm protecting from the storm thought all the whip's or pain you but me you did out of love. But most of all I want to wish you a happy birthday of lovin' me.

Part of Tia's emotional landscape involved her ability to identify with her mother's role as a disciplinarian. Along similar lines of Tia's identity with and adoration of her mother, Kecia wrote about texting her mother for consolation over boyfriend problems she was having in the midst of a school day. Kecia wrote,

I broke up wit my boyfriend because his girlfriend called me and text me I got mad then I made them mad I was happy to break up wit him. My mom said he was not a good boyfriend. I am waiting on the right boy to come around to treat me right. I text my mom during school she text me back. I am daddy little girl and I will always be.

In a piece about McDonald's toys, Felicia gave her mother credit for not allowing her to eat at McDonalds more than once a week, which she felt kept her from getting fat.

Mc.Donalds *TOYS*

I think Mc.Donalds give toys to the kids so that they can always keep going. You no I think that that is a pretty good Idea!! I like to get toys from Mc.Donald ,but not only me my friends do too! The funny thing is were all 14!!ha-ha.
You know the bad thing about Mc.Donalds is that there food is not so healthy. It is really bad for you because there is so much sugar. My mom lets me eat it like once a week because she watches over me and make sure I am healthy. I wouldn't blame them people for getting so big because if it wasn't for my mom I would be as fat as them. (Oh crap now I got to knock on wood)

Moving beyond Felicia's pragmatic gratitude for her mother's rules, Adrianna offered homage to her mother through a piece that depicted lofty adoration for her mother.

God Creation
Only god can make a mom he does it all the time.
He put in to the love of a moms heart a special warmth and gentleness touch of your
mom love only god can make a moms trust the one that give hope and laughter to
the children of the lord that ones dried your tears and your mom that will always
keep loving you to those that have a mom have to stop and whisper thank you lord
for my lovely grateful mom.

Mimicking tones of a Mother's Day greeting card, writing such as Adrianna's captured the ways the girls folded in images of motherhood present in various popular culture texts. Indeed, such socially cultivated depictions of motherhood offered the girls symbols to ponder and integrate into their personal experiences with being mothered. As such, part of the emotional tangle of writing to, for, and about mothers entailed numerous metaphors and stereotypes of motherhood the girls were exposed to in addition to their own experiences.

By turns, all of the girls described having a quasi-peer relationship with their mothers in which they would side with their mothers over their stepfathers/fathers, keep secrets with and from their mothers, present themselves as less naive than their mothers, and talk to their mothers as if they were their siblings. Secrecy played a role in many of these scenarios. The primary secret the girls kept from their mothers involved boys they were dating or were romantically interested in. Kiara captured the mismatch in knowledge about dating activities between the girls and their mothers when she told me with sarcasm her mother's dating rules. "Mom said, when I'm ready for a boyfriend to tell her, and she will give me the little speech. I'm like I don't want the speech. I already know the speech." Kiara had been "dating" boys secretly for two years when she told me about her mother's plans for "the speech." Sometimes dating relationships were only kept secret from the girls' fathers. In such instances mothers functioned as a confidant for their daughters. For example, Kecia stated in an interview, "I'm not allowed to date, but I tell my mom about it. My mom told me to wait until I'm fifteen to tell my dad." Similarly, Veronica, who did not know her father, declared she could tell her mother anything and quoted her mother's reasoning of why she really needed a mother more than a father when she stated, "A mom could be two parts: a mom and a dad but a dad could never be a mom." Of all the girls in the group, Veronica depicted her relationship with her mother as being the most peer-like.

Sometimes the role of confidant turned into a role reversal between a mother and daughter. For instance, Jenni wrote about a typical day in her life involving routines in which she took on some of the adult responsibilities of mothering.

wake up
c what time it is
take a shower
put my clothes on
turn on my straighten
straighten my hair
wake up my mom
tell her to turn on the car
wake up my brother to get ready then
we go to school
go to the oudotorian
to go furst period
than all my periods
bell rings to get out
go get somthin to eat
go home
brush my teeth

In all of these examples of writing to, for, and about mothers the girls were trying to carve out common ground with their mothers through a shared experience, knowledge, privilege, or concern. Within this search for common ground, more often than not the girls' narratives consisted of a gaping absence of any maternal influence or meaningful connections with their mothers.

The Maternal Void

Within the mother-daughter continuum, most of the girls characterized their relationship with their mothers as existing at the end of the continuum where mothers were virtually absent from their daughters' lives. Because references to their mothers were typically missing from the girls' writing in the group and in other venues such as their *MySpace* pages, often it seemed to me mothers were little more than a vague outline fading in the distance on the horizon of childhood memories. Even when mothers did make an appearance in one of these writing venues, the details were often obscured clichés. For instance, Alicia wrote a caption that read, "MY MOM AND ME" underneath a picture of another girl hugging a mother on her *MySpace* page, which had the effect of creating a façade of her actual relationship with her mother. Mothers were so absent from the girls' Discourse and narratives within the group and in their writing that I was often surprised when one of the girls mentioned something about her mother, showed me a picture of her mother, or wrote about her mother.

If I asked the girls about their mothers, they all had plenty of information to share. With the exception of Isabel, the girls had studied their mothers for years and knew well how to anticipate their mothers' approval and anger, yet virtually all of them stated they wished they had a closer relationship with their mothers. Unfortunately, in most difficult incidents with boys or fighting at school, the girls functioned without maternal input. Mothers were somewhere in the periphery of the girls' lives, but they were not in the moments at the mall, or at the movie theater, or the skating rink, or in the sixth grade hallway, or in the writing group. Even in a scenario like Isabel's where as a sixth grader she wrote odes to a mother who had stepped in and out of her life and whom she craved to know, through middle school most of the girls' mothers increasingly faded from their view as an audience or subject for their writing. As such, mothers existed in some ill-defined territory beyond the purview of the writing group.

Ironically, research such as Kerpelman, Shoffner, and Ross-Griffin's (2002) highlights the critical role mothers play in helping African American adolescent girls develop positive "possible selves" and strategies for achieving academic success (see also Usher-Seriki, Bynum, & Callands, 2008). Similarly, Thomas and King (2011) noted the important role that African American mothers' messages send to their daughters with respect to a positive "gendered racial socialization" (p. 138). In their study, through interview and questionnaire data, Thomas and King found:

> The majority of [mothers'] responses focused on teaching their daughters self-determination and assertiveness (19.5%). Mothers also focused on helping daughters develop self-pride (15% of responses). Mothers in the study emphasized the importance of being respectful of others and recognizing equality (8.5%). Responses also focused on male-female relationships (7.3%), the importance of spirituality and religious beliefs (9.7%), racial pride (7.3%), and cultural heritage and legacy (85%). (p. 139)

Overall, the girls in Thomas and King's study developed a sense of psychological strength about their cultural identities and gender from their mothers. As the authors pointed out, such messages are especially critical in a society imbued with numerous dead-ended stereotypes for ethnic minority adolescent girls marked with considerable levels of racism and sexism.

In another study, Euro-American mothers' messages were also found to bear significance for pubescent girls' development of positive self-esteem, body image, and gender role identity (Usmiani & Daniluk, 1997). In fact, research across the lifespan within varying socio-economic and ethnic backgrounds supports the notion that mother-daughter relationships are so interdependent and entail a kind of "mutual" mothering that daughters become like their mothers (Boyd, 1989, p. 292). Whether such relationships are developed through unconscious identification or principles of modeling has been the subject of debate within psychoanalytic and social learning theories (Boyd, 1989). While many theorists have put forth the idea that daughters struggle to both identify with and separate from their mothers into adulthood (e.g., Bojczyk, Lehan, McWey, Melson, & Kaufman, 2011), mother-daughter relationships are nonetheless predicated upon mutual social and physical origins and commonalities that never completely cease to exist within a daughter's journey towards autonomy. Given the power of the mother-daughter relationship, I found it concerning that mothers were backgrounded in the girls' writing and Discourse during a time when the girls needed nurturing through the daily realities they were contending with.

Implications for Writing Pedagogy

The number one reason girls reported not sharing writing with their mothers had to do with their fear of getting into trouble for what they wrote. They were afraid their mothers would censor their stories and admonish them for their perspectives. In essence, the girls were afraid of being judged by their mothers, so they created private spaces beyond the maternal gaze for writing. Adolescent girls' inclination towards such hidden writing outside of school needs to be cultivated in school in ways that retain the girls' privacy and ownership. Pedagogically, fostering the same impulse to write that Felicia described requires teachers to permit students to engage in a lot of writing no one (e.g., teachers, parents, peers) will ever read—unless the girls choose otherwise. As discussed in previous chapters, adolescent girls need to have numerous writing experiences that are free from the fear of external critique.

At the same time that adolescent girls need freedom from judgment about their writing, they also need guidance in social issues they confront and reflect on through writing. In essence, they need empathic readers who can offer guidance without the weight of judgment to help fill the maternal void many adolescent girls experience. As such, teachers need to serve as an audience that can provide respite from criticism while guiding the girls through broader social issues such as racism and sexism. Mary Blalock articulated this notion as "A Bill of Rights for Girls" (2000) in which she highlighted the following rights:

> The right to like yourself, the right to like your body, the right to have your cake and eat it too, the right to get angry, the right to feel protected, the right to develop your brain, the right to be yourself around boys, and the right to your own role models. (pp. 75–76)

Such rights or alternative perspectives need to be presented to adolescent girls as they contend with an understanding of what it means to be female in contemporary society through their writing. Adolescent girls need adult female role models who write with, to, and for them. If they cannot find these role models in their mothers, then they need to read writing by other female role models, and they need to be nurtured in their efforts to create their own gendered and raced writing at school.

Concluding Vignette: Have You Told Your Mom This?

Veronica was the only girl in the group who stated definitively that she and her mom were completely honest with each other. Veronica explained,

> Me and my mom are really close because I could sit there and tell her anything I need to like even if it's like I don't feel like I should tell her. We don't have no se-crets. If she has a problem, she'll tell me. We just share.

While Veronica and her mother had created a relationship where they could be completely honest with each other, most of the girls were still trying to define this elusive common ground with their mothers.

Every time one of the girls in the group told me about a new boyfriend, I asked them, "Does your mom know?" More often than not, the girls stated their mothers did not know or knew only partial truths about the boy. On one hand, some of this adolescent secrecy about crushes on boys was to be expected. On the other hand, some of the secrets the girls wrote about—like feeling confused about their gender identity or being molested by a stepfa-ther—were much more serious and were part of the treacherous end of the mother-daughter continuum the girls were trying to navigate. As Felicia stated, the girls had to ascertain if their writing was "too personal" to share with their mothers. Consequently, the girls packaged much of their lives and their writing into concealed pages. Sometimes the girls not only kept secrets from their mothers that eked out in their writing, but like Felicia they also kept secrets with their mothers from fathers, teachers, peers, and Child Protective Services. Such secrecy from so many directions served to push the girls further away from an audience for their writing and deepen their invisibility within and beyond school.

References

Blalock, M. (2000). A bill of rights for girls. In L. Christensen (Ed.), *Reading, writing, and rising up: Teaching about social justice and the power of the written word.* (pp. 75–76). Milwaukee, WI: Rethinking Schools.

Bojczyk, K., Lehan, T., McWey, L., Melson, G., & Kaufman, D. (2011). Mothers' and their adult daughters' perceptions of their relationship. *Journal of Family Issues, 32* (4), 452–481.

Boyd, C. (1989). Mothers and daughters: A discussion of theory and research. *Journal of Marriage and the Family, 51* (2), 291–301.

Hirsch, M. (1981). Mothers and daughters. *Signs: Journal of Women in Culture and Society, 7* (11), 200–222.

Kerpelman, J., Shoffner, M., & Ross-Griffin, S. (2002). African American mothers' and daughters' beliefs about possible selves and their strategies for reaching the adolescents' future academic and career goals. *Journal of Youth and Adolescence, 31* (4), 289–302.

Meeus, W., Iedema, J., Maassen, G., & Engels, R. (2005). Separation-individuation revisited: On the interplay of parent-adolescent relations, identity and emotional adjustment in adolescence. *Journal of Adolescence, 28* (1), 89–106.

Rich, A. (1976). *Of woman born: Motherhood as experience and institution.* New York, NY: W. W. Norton & Co.

Thomas, A., & King, C. (2011). Gendered racial socialization of African American mothers and daughters. *The Family Journal: Counseling and Therapy for Couples and Families, 15* (2), 137–142.

Usher-Seriki, K, Bynum, M., & Callands, T. (2008). Mother-daughter communication about sex and sexual intercourse among middle-to-upper-class african american girls. *Journal of Family Issues, 29* (7), 901–917.

Usmiani, S., & Daniluk, J. (1997). Mothers and their adolescent daughters: Relationship between self-esteem, gender role identity, and body image. *Journal of Youth and Adolescence, 26* (1), 45–62.

Chapter Seven

"I Have to Remember It's Writing and Not Texting": Composing on the Other Side of the Digital Divide

Narrative Profile of Kiara

Kiara was a long-limbed Latina girl with a bright smile and penetrating gaze who appeared in the writing group at the beginning of seventh grade. Kiara joined the group because she was inseparable from her best friend, Felicia, who had become a member of the group the previous year. In seventh grade, Kiara always sat next to Felicia, peered over her shoulder to read her writing, and talked with her constantly in whispered giggles behind a bank of computers. On rare occasions, Kiara poked her head up from her computer to assert an opinion or defend Felicia from other girls' comments in the group. Because Kiara typically kept herself tucked behind Felicia engaged in giddy dialogue, moments where she emerged and spoke to another girl or to me with somber intensity surprised me initially. Through time, however, I came to see Kiara's piercing observations as merely another facet to her otherwise light hearted and shy personality.

In seventh grade, Kiara took many cues about writing in the group from Felicia and often wrote pieces about their friendship such as the following:

My BFF   Felicia

My bff felicia has taught me so much for example like when people talk about me she told me "so what they must be jealous". That goes to say that my BFF always picks me up when I am down.
  The End

In seventh grade, Kiara's style of writing drifted between diary entries and *MySpace* aphorisms derived from the universal truths of anonymous authors. Kiara also often included cut and pasted images from the Internet to enhance the print text of her writing. In the following example, Kiara combined a well-known saying with an image from the Internet to construct her own version of the text.

"Kiara's Heart Poem"

HeARt
YoUR HeArT Js nOt tO PLAy wJTh,
YoUr HeArt iS nOt A toY,
BuT iF yOu wANt Jt brOKeN,
ThAn gⁱᵛ¹ iT To A BoY

By juxtaposing the print with billowy, floating hearts, Kiara added another interpretive layer to the text that served to reconstruct the bitter dating persona present in the words. This writing also captured the juxtaposition of Kiara's child-like nature with her often hardened outlook on the motives of other people.

In seventh grade, there were many days when Kiara "had no ideas for writing" and thus spent most of her time joking with Felicia, surfing the Internet, and coming up with a last minute piece such as the following:

> TODAY I AM IN RIGHTING CLASS AND I WAS SUPPOSE TO WRITE LIKE 30 MIN AGO BUT I WANTED TO PLAY SOLITARIE AND MOW I ONLY GOT 5 MIN LEFT SO NOW I AM COMIN UP WITH THIS STORY AND NOW I RAN OUT OF THINGS TO SAY I GUESS I AM DONE BYE.

Although Kiara entered the group as a less-than-serious writer adhered to her best friend, Felicia, through weeks of observing Felicia write, talking quietly with me about her writing, and exploring websites on the computer Kiara realized the writing group was a place where she could talk and write about real things and began to write more incisive stories about her life such as the following.

Snuck off

> Today I snuck off cause like I was suppose to be in my choir class but I didn't want to because like I like choir but she is mean some times but I would never tell her that because I love her she is like a best friend to me

Little by little Kiara stopped writing about her "B.F.F.," writing about not
writing, and reiterating adopted words from the Internet. Over time, Kiara's
life increasingly became the subject of her compositions as in the following
piece:

The cool day

**Today was cool cuz no one got mad at me for any thing. And everyone was
being nice to me. Plus there's this boy I like and I found out that he likes me to.
He is so cute cuz he is little. But that's not the only reason I like him cuz he is
the funniest boy that I know. Well let's change the subject cuz that is getting
old. Ha! Lol! Well any way today was also cool because I am in the writing club
as u can tell. Ha! Ha! Well I am out of words to say. Oh wait a minute im not
out of words cuz I forgot to mention that I sat with my friend felicia at lunch
today**

And we almost got in trouble like 100 times

From somewhat playful writing such as this, Kiara eventually began to write
about deeper issues in her life.

In March of her seventh grade year, I asked Kiara who she wrote to
when she composed text in the writing group. "I write like it's a diary,"
Kiara responded.

"So are you writing to yourself?"' I asked.

Kiara shrugged and stated, "I dunno. What does that mean, 'write to
yourself?"

"That's how most diaries are written—to one's self," I tried to explain.

"I guess so," Kiara answered and then quickly returned her gaze to the
computer screen.

At the end of her seventh grade year, Kiara noted the importance of writing
as a way "to express yourself" privately because "you don't have to tell
anybody about it; you just write it down." Kiara also emphasized the importance of writing "true stories," stating, "If it didn't happen, don't write it."

In eighth grade, Kiara returned to the writing group taller, more pensive,
and without her trademark hoop earrings. In eighth grade Kiara stopped
being friends with Felicia, took up with other girls outside of the writing
group she could "trust," and became much more focused on writing about the
truth of her life and the dismal circumstances she often observed around her.
In eighth grade, Kiara's demeanor became more caustic, and she spoke more
frequently about instances of inequity that bothered her, such as the ways
boys treated girls at school. While trust continued to be of great concern for
Kiara, in eighth grade, attending the writing group became more about giving
voice to real-life events than catering to or fighting with friends. Truth and
getting to the heart of issues became a constant pursuit for Kiara as a writer
and a member of the writing group. At one point Kiara coached Amber to tell

me what was bothering her by stating with unbending sincerity, "It's ok, you can trust her."

On a field trip to the university to hear several children and adolescent literature authors speak about their writing, Kiara was given a children's book about frogs by Nic Bishop (2008). Kiara spent much of the morning pouring over the book fascinated by the nonfiction topics and the highly focused, visually intense images. The piercing nonfiction text and images in Bishop's book reminded me of Kiara's burgeoning style of writing where image carried equal importance to the print such as in the following example:

"All Things Are One" by Issac Abrams

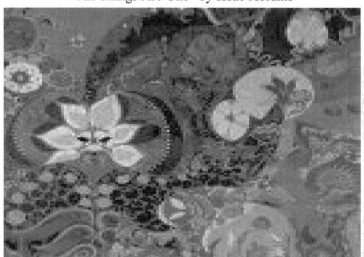

I chose this picture because it is like me. Beautiful colors, bright, crazy and much more!!!

Writing such as this illustrated the ways text and image were often two halves of the same process of composing for Kiara. Images were also a way to encode meaning. Like all of the girls in the group, Kiara did not want to be judged as a writer by her audience. Thus, incorporating images with her writing allowed Kiara a sense of interpretive privacy. Kiara noted similar benefits about using text messaging language in writing.

While Kiara did not view texting on her cell phone as "correct" writing, she did note the time-saving features of using the shorthand language common in texting (e.g., "r" for "are"). Even with this perspective, Kiara stated she sometimes had to remind herself not to use text messaging language in her writing at school. She also stated using text messaging language in a handwritten note in school was convenient if the note was intercepted by teachers because they had no idea what the note said. Thus, Kiara reasoned that even though texting language was not correct, it was a great way to include and exclude an audience.

As part of a discussion about text messaging language, Kiara instructed me to "Type 304" on my cell phone and "turn it upside down." Before I had time to fish out my phone, Kiara quickly explained 304 turned into the word "hoe." "Oh, yes, I get it. So, if you call a girl a 304 you're really calling her a whore?" I asked. "Yes," Kiara giggled and added most people do not know what you're saying. In this exchange, Kiara gave me a lesson in not only the latest slang circulating the school to identify a girl as a whore, but also she provided me with a profound example of the ways adolescents create their own subculture of language, replicate dominant ideologies about gender, and assert power—in this case over other girls. This example also illustrated the ways digital media facilitate the creation of new language and how the use of this language defines membership in a particular Discourse community. Stated differently, this example demonstrated how information and communication technologies (ICTs) change the ways literacy is practiced (Coiro, Knobel, Lankshear, & Leu, 2008, p. 17).

New Literacies

The writing the girls produced within the writing group was sprinkled with several trappings from their participation in digital media. More specifically, the girls' writing contained pieces of multimodal text, text message Discourse, the rhetorical structure of social media, and digital identity performance (Thomas, 2004). In this manner, the girls' participation in New Literacies outside of the writing group spilled over into their writing within the writing group (Coiro, Knobel, Lankshear, & Leu, 2008).

At the dawn of the new millennium, the New London Group (2000) published a seminal work entitled *Multiliteracies: Literacy Learning and the Design of Social Futures* that became a cornerstone to the emerging field of New Literacies theory (Cope & Kalantzis, 2009). The New London Group's (2000) "pedagogy of multiliteracies" emerged primarily from an expanded notion of what constituted text that entailed a dynamic interplay between multiple modalities, multiple sign systems, and linguistic and cultural diversity (p. 9). They defined multiliteracies as:

> Six elements in the meaning-making process: those of Linguistic Meaning, Visual Meaning, Audio Meaning, Gestural Meaning, Spatial Meaning, and the Multimodal patterns of meaning that relate the first five modes of meaning to each other. (p. 7)

From the time the New London Group (2000) constructed a "pedagogy of multiliteracies," the Internet has evolved in ways that have deepened and extended this original framework (Cope & Kalantzis, 2009; Gee, 2009). Nested within multiple social and cultural practices, the Internet offers numerous examples of multiliteracies and thus is a driving force of New Literacies theory.

New Literacies theory represents a paradigm shift for literacy researchers from a stance of viewing literacy as a largely isolated "event" that produces print-based text to a stance of viewing literacy as a "practice" that is participatory, dynamic, representative of linguistic and cultural diversity, and grounded in "socially inscribed" interactions (Lewis & Fabos, 2005, p. 474). New Literacies theory is a compilation of multiliteracies, critical literacy, youth culture, postmodernism, popular culture, and a rapidly growing panoply of digital literacies (Coiro, Knobel, Lankshear, & Leu, 2008; Gee, 2009; Street, 2003). Coiro, Knobel, Lankshear, and Leu (2008) noted,

> New literacies are identified with an epochal change in technologies and associated changes in social and cultural ways of doing things, ways of being, and ways of viewing the world. (p. 27)

In other words, "New technologies require new social practices and new literacies" (Coiro, Knobel, Lankshear, & Leu, 2008, p. 6). Thus, New Literacies studies strive to keep pace with identifying and analyzing emerging information and communication technologies (ICTs).

In 2008 Coiro, Knobel, Lankshear, and Leu published the *Handbook of Research on New Literacies*, which the editors argued was largely to bring some cohesion to the sprawling and deictic literacies emerging during the first decade in the 21st Century. Both prior to and since the publication of this book, numerous books on the topic of New Literacies have been published and studies have been conducted on various aspects of New Literacies largely driven by the explosion of easily accessible information and new genres of text on the Internet in the 21st Century (Alvermann, 2010; Hagood, 2009; Knobel & Lankshear, 2010; Thomas, 2007). In reference to this growing body of research, Leu, O'Bryne, Zawilinski, McVerry, and Everett-Cacopardo (2009) concluded, "New Literacies are multifaceted, and our understanding of them benefits from multiple points of view" (p. 266).

Studies concerned with emerging writing practices spawned by new technologies have similarly created a new frontier for literacy practitioners to explore. In a policy report, Blake Yancey (2009), past president for NCTE, posited,

Today, in the 21st Century, people write as never before—in print and online. We thus face three challenges that are also opportunities: developing new *models of writing*; designing a *new curriculum* supporting those models; and creating *models for teaching* that curriculum. (p. 1, emphasis in the original)

In 21st-Century writing, Blake Yancey added, "Composers become composers not through direct and formal instruction (if at all), but rather through what we might call an extracurricular co-apprenticeship" (p. 4). Other researchers have referred to this kind of writing as "self-sponsored" writing (Haas, Takayoshi, Carr, Hudson, & Pollock, 2011) and participatory media (Guzzetti, Elliott, & Welsch, 2010). For example, Haas, Takayoshi, Carr, Hudson, and Pollock (2011) studied middle- and working-class college students engaged in IM (instant messaging) discussions to examine the "written language features of IM" and how such "self-sponsored" texts were constructed within Discourse communities or "in situ" (pp. 379, 380). Through an examination of a 32,000-word corpus, Haas, Takayoshi, Carr, Hudson, and Pollock argued that while the larger purpose of the IM texts was social or phatic in nature as opposed to being informational, this nonetheless did not negate the prevalent features of IM such as metamarkings, which indicated self-conscious acts of writing. The authors described IM as "writing pulled in the direction of speech . . . which attempts to inscribe the paralinguistic" (p. 397). They concluded with the directive that mediated text should be considered legitimate forms of writing because IM, text messages, *Facebook* updates, Tweets on *Twitter*, and the like are all "purposefully constructed of visible marks in graphic space" (p. 398).

In another study involving an examination of IM as a literacy practice, Lewis and Fabos (2005) found adolescents viewed IM as contingent upon their social status and ability to be an "insider" as a participant with respect to elements of language use and timing of responses. Lewis and Fabos added, "Participants viewed their entire IM sessions—including simultaneous sessions that often lasted for hours—not as individual, separate exchanges but as a larger entwined narrative" (p. 493). Thus, the authors concluded viewing IM as a written text or isolated literacy event offered little application to school purposes for writing. Conversely, the authors noted viewing IM as a literacy practice imbued with social and cultural moves and meanings offered a great deal more connection to classroom literacy practices. Drawing a similar conclusion, Angela Thomas (2004) studied an online graphical chat environment to observe how girls used words and images to create a digital presence as a type of performed writing. Thomas called this deliberate use of words and images "identity performance" and argued, "linguistic variations of cybertalk are directly related to identity performance" (p. 367). Of such writing, Thomas also concluded, "the command of the words that shape the self in this space" gave the girls "power" (p. 380).

Similar digital media for writing to the ones described in the above studies were available to the girls in the computer lab at school, on their personal computers at home, and on their cell phones. Their use of them, however, was more reminiscent of the "girl number 20" metaphor from feminist research that is based on a character from Dickens's novel *Hard Times* who is intellectually diminished by her teacher and chorus of peers (Gonick, 2007). Like the interchangeable "girl number 20," much of the girls' online writing practices replicated dominant Discourses that blurred their identities with media-driven stereotypes.

The Digital Divide

While information and communication technologies offer numerous compelling and evolving applications for New Literacies (e.g., *YouTube, Live Journal*), several researchers have also noted participation in such rapidly changing contexts is contingent upon the extent to which individuals have access to technology. This concern has been referred to as the "digital divide" wherein disparities of knowledge exist between individuals who have access to ICTs and those who do not (Cullen, 2001). Coiro, Knobel, Lankshear, and Leu (2008) observed, "New literacies will continuously be new, multiple, and rapidly disseminated," making it challenging to keep pace with ICTs (p. 24). For such reasons, access to technology is increasingly viewed as a human necessity akin to access to clean water. In 2009, the Constitution Council in France "declared access to the Internet to be a basic human right" (Times Online, Retrieved May 27, 2011 from http://technology.timesonline. co.uk/tol/news/tech_and_web/article6478542.ece). Citing a similar connection between access to information and civic participation, Hobbs (2010) argued, "Media and digital literacy education is now fundamentally implicated in the practice of citizenship" and further noted the Knight Commission described the necessity of media literacy for citizens in a democracy as "digital citizenship" (Hobbs, 2010, p. 16).

Access to ICTs is also viewed as a gender and social class issue (e.g., Guzzetti, Elliott, & Welsch, 2010). Nearly two decades ago Lather (1992) observed, "The profound effect that electronic mediation exerts on the way we perceive ourselves and reality is occurring in a world marked by gross maldistribution of power and resources" (p. 88). More recently, Coiro, Knobel, Lankshear, and Leu (2008) asked whether ICTs help *all* individuals to "fully realize their potential as global citizens in the 21st Century" (p. 17). With respect to gender, Gonick (2007) noted of digital media, "New discursive spaces for girls to enter as subjects . . . are contradictory spaces acting as both leverage for change as well as a closure on what it is possible to become" (p. 439). In our media-saturated world, it is difficult to not have some knowledge of ICTs. The digital divide in the United States, thus, is not so much about general access to the Internet, as such technology is increasingly available in schools and public libraries, but rather about how such access is utilized to promote full civic participation. Some of this utilization is about the availability of cutting-edge technology (e.g., high-speed Internet, Skype-equipped laptops, cell phone applications), but some of this utilization is about the tools of critical thinking (Leu, O'Byrne, Zawilinski, McVerry, & Everett-Cacopardo, 2009) and identity performances (Thomas, 2004) that individuals bring to technology. Political action and revolutions have been launched through participatory media on the Internet—for some.

The Girls' Use of Technology for Self-Directed Composing

A year and a half into the project, I surveyed the girls about their use of ICTs and found that the majority of them did not have cell phones or access to a computer with the Internet at home. One year later, I asked the girls again about their access to technology and learned their access had increased. Every girl stated she had access to a cell phone, which she used to send text messages to friends and family. A few of the girls had access to the Internet on their cell phones. Only two girls did not have a computer with Internet access at home for financial reasons. And, one girl was not allowed to participate in the social networking website *MySpace*. The girls who had Internet access at home and were permitted to use *MySpace* reported using the Internet primarily for *MySpace*. Only one girl stated she used the Internet to help her complete homework. At school, the girls could not access *MySpace* or *YouTube,* but they could locate information about celebrities on other websites that were not blocked and listen to some of their favorite pop music online and on their MP3 players. They could also engage in IM through an internal program at the school. Generally, however, the girls did not use the school's IM program. I observed three of the girls participate sporadically in the school's IM program during the writing group. Text messaging on cell phones was a much more portable and consistent way to send electronic messages to friends. The girls had never heard of blogs, *Twitter*, or wikis. They similarly reported that no participatory media applications were utilized in their classes even though the school the girls attended had its own internal instant messenger system, computer lab, computers in the library, and a way for students to create digital archives of their writing.

The impulse to create multimodal texts was strong for all of the girls in the group. To varying degrees they all experimented with fonts, color, and images in their writing. Much of this was reminiscent of their *MySpace* pages that were filled with images, sounds, movement, and multimedia hypertext links. The more multimodal elements were present in their writing, the more their writing was driven by an imagined social context and audience involving friends. Much of this writing was reminiscent of the rhetorical structure of *MySpace* and phatic in nature or similar to speech acts that served purely social purposes.

In terms of the girls' writing practices involving the use of ICTs, one of the girls viewed text messaging on her phone as a form of writing because it was a way to "start a conversation with someone," like other forms of writing, and because she had written a poem on a text message that her friends had forwarded around until it came back to her, like the numerous poems and aphorisms that are perpetually circulated on *MySpace.* The girls all used text messaging language such as IDK, LOL, JK, and IDC in text messages, on *MySpace* posts, and on occasion in their writing in the group. They described the use of such language as necessary for their participation in peer Discourse communities. In fact, several of the girls stated they disliked such text messaging jargon but used it in order to fit in with their friends. Even with these applications of technology, the girls viewed composing text as done separately from computer use and preferably at home with pen and paper. The girls shied away from writing too much original prose on *MySpace* because they had learned to rein in their opinions from previous experiences involving unpleasant feedback from their "friends list" readers. Veronica blogged on *MySpace* once; Isabel blogged on *MySpace* twice. Both girls subsequently completely abandoned this form of writing. Most of the girls' writing on *MySpace*, consequently, consisted of downloaded comments from linked websites such as "MyHotComments.com," brief descriptions and updates about themselves, brief comments to friends, and brief captions beneath pictures they uploaded. Even so, *MySpace* was the epicenter of the girls' digital composing worlds. The girls engaged in e-mail only through this account, if at all. Several of the girls were not even aware of the e-mail function on *MySpace* until I pointed it out. Instead, they communicated to friends on a daily (even hourly) basis through the ranking of their friends list and the "mood" and "status" updates they posted about themselves on *MySpace*. Such updates were scrutinized and often used to engage in both fights and reconciliations with friends and boyfriends.

MySpace Ideologies and Identity Performance

With the exception of Alicia, the girls posted numerous pictures of themselves on their *MySpace* pages. Many of these pictures were posed to look like the photos of celebrities they idolized (e.g., wearing sunglasses and smiling). There were also many pictures of the girls hugging their friends, pictures of select family members (i.e., usually siblings or cousins, never fathers and very rarely mothers), pictures of their favorite celebrities, and pictures of boys they knew. Alicia chose only images of celebrities from the Internet to put on her *MySpace* page and perpetually referred to one of the celebrities as herself with tacked-on captions like "Me looking sexy." Thomas (2004) explained this kind of visual role playing as "the combination of the performance of one's desires and fantasies coupled with the voyeuristic-like gaze at that performance" (p. 376). *MySpace* fed the girls' creative, multimodal impulse with composing through the graphics, background images, and music they included, but such text also often kept them mired in sexist ideations and personas.

If the girls did not use their real names for their pages on *MySpace*, the names they created for themselves depicted infantilized and sexualized personas such as "!$*$SEXY CH!CK*$!," "[MaMmAs]," and "B@BY K." The names of other female friends listed on the girls' *MySpace* pages also included angry personas and thus offered a slightly wider range of female personas as depicted in the following examples:

> **-...sinG1e...-**
> PhUCK LoVE
> Nick's Wifey
> D!V@l!C()U$
> RoXY FoXXY
> %I DON'T WONT YO (SIDE HOE) I WANT U MAIN (BITCH)
> UR A LUCKY MOTHER FUCKER 2 KNOW ME
> *~I'm his ride or die chick~*

All of the constructed names of either the girls' or their female friends ran the gamut from cute to tough and virtually all contained sexual overtones. Boys' made up names on *MySpace* who were "friends" with the girls in the group were often just as textually playful and sexualized, but they also frequently imparted an aggressive and even oppressive persona such as the following examples:

> $BIG PIMP$
> D@ Bo$$
> D_1_&_ONLY

M@N FUCK @LL TH3 HO3Z Now D@YZ CUZ TH3Y @!NT SH!T
I jus cnt pik 1 so u can never say I'm choosy hoez

Sex appeal was a primary focus of the games, bulletins, and comments the girls participated in on *MySpace*. For example, their pages were filled with "Kiss Me/I Just Kissed You" comments and "Do you like me?" queries often accompanied by a provocative picture. The girls also downloaded statements from MyHotComments.com that presented edgy quips about dating and competition such as the following poem that was posted on Veronica's *MySpace* page in the fall of her eighth grade year.

YOU CALL ME A SLUT
LIKE IT'S ACTUALLY TRUE
I'M SORRY
SKANK
I'M NOT YOU

Thus, with the propagation of text such as this, the discursive context of *MySpace* promoted a narrow range of gender roles for the girls to adopt, which the girls not only copied and pasted into their pages but also replicated with the names they selected for themselves and the captions, however brief, they wrote. Alicia constructed an imaginary narrative about her life with sexy celebrity pictures along with the following captions she created:

i just got my hair done
me going out with my gurls
me going 2 work
me looking mad cause they took a picture of me [in a bikini]
me in my kar
me taking a home picture I look a hot mess!!!!
me looking sexy like always
me trying 2 look cute like always
me looking hot
me posing
me on my ex car

Collectively, the celebrity pictures combined with the captions created a performance identity for Alicia as a young woman who was "sexy like always." Such ideologies pertaining to dating roles and gender identity were the driving force in the girls' literacy practices on *MySpace*. Although some examples demonstrated a desire to disrupt passive, "good girl" gender roles, most of the girls' identity performances (Thomas, 2004) on *MySpace* served to replicate traditional ideologies surrounding gender and dating roles where girls are expected to be sexually attractive and fawn over boys. For example,

Erica posted "i love my boo!!" in big sparkling bright red letters next to the following "mood" update about a boy's behavior towards her:

HESZ
TRYINqq so
HARDD IHH
THNKK IHH
SHUDD qIVE
HIM AHH CHANCE
4 ITT, , , WATT
YUHH THINKK????

Isabel wrote in her "mood": "*I love chris*" beneath her update where she wrote: "omg cant believe me n my baby gonna spend valentine together ☺ ugh cant wait." Even though the girls had "the command of the words that shape the self in this space," much of the girls' power was given over to the strictures of acceptable dating roles for females (Thomas, 2004, p. 380). Examples of posts and "mood" updates such as these demonstrate the extent to which the girls needed opportunities for critically framing much of the text on *MySpace* in order to develop "a critical knowing of ideology" within this online environment (Gonick, 2007, p. 437).

New Literacies In and Out of School

Although the girls' access to technology had increased over their years in middle school, it was nonetheless largely relegated to texting on their cell phones and posting updates on *MySpace*. While there were many technological skills the girls acquired in such digital environments, I nonetheless wondered what access to these technologies and the Internet truly netted the girls in terms of the extent to which they were encouraged to participate in the democratizing potential of New Literacies. In other words, did these ICTs give the girls a voice that was unavailable to them through school literacy practices or other First Space settings they participated in?

One of the distinguishing points of 21st-Century literacy practices is for individuals to see themselves as not just consumers of literacy but also producers of literacy (Greenhow, Robelia, & Hughes, 2009; Leu, O'Byrne, Zawilinski, McVerry, & Everett-Cacopardo, 2009). To some extent the girls had mastered becoming producers of text with their use of digital social networking media (e.g., *MySpace*).Whether participation in such social media encouraged "full civic, economic, and personal participation in a world community," however, is under debate (Coiro, Knobel, Lankshear, &

Leu, 2008, p. 41). For instance, Leu et. al. (2009) noted of adolescents' online practices,

> Although adolescent "digital natives" may be skilled with social networking, tex-ting, video downloads, MP3 downloads, and mash ups, they are not generally skilled with online information use, including locating and critically evaluating in-formation. (p. 266)

Thus, Leu et. al., found being technologically savvy did not automatically lead to sophisticated critical thinking skills. Similarly, in a longitudinal study examining whether providing students from low-income families with computer access at home improved their academic performance at school, Vigdor and Ladd (2010) discovered supplying students with home computer technology was "associated with modest but statistically significant and persistent negative impacts on student math and reading test scores" (p. iii).

Another piece to the debate about whether the Internet is beneficial for adolescents is the extent to which social media literacy practices carry over into academic expectations for literacy (Bean, Readance, & Baldwin, 2008; Beers, 2007; Burke, 2007). Much of this issue hinges upon how one defines and evaluates literacy tasks. Consider Tara's introduction on her *MySpace* page during her eighth grade year:

> NAME BE TARA T 4 SHORT SPORTS IS MY LIFE I LOVE SHOPPING AND HANGING WITH THE BESTIES I HAVE A TONE OF BESTIES BUT THE MAIN ONE IS KIMEE SHE IS THE ONLY ONE I TELL JUST ABOUT EVERYTHING . . .. I AM A CHRISTIAN. . .IF U DNT LIKE ME I COULD CARE LESS . . . IF U WANT TO KNW ANYTHING ABOUT NE JUST ASK . . . BYE

When I've shared this writing with teacher candidates, I have received comments critiquing the value and relevance to academic literacy tasks of this type of writing common in social networking sites such as *MySpace.* The teacher candidates largely viewed Tara's writing as a collection of slang knitted loosely together in a series of incomplete sentences that combined to form one long, run-on sentence. A closer analysis of the writing within the context of the site, however, yields a more complex understanding of the literacy skills present in this writing.

Beneath the glaring grammatical "mistakes" in Tara's writing lay her intention to assert a quasi-bully identity through her use of direct language, all capital letters, and somewhat confrontational tone, "IF U DNT LIKE ME I COULD CARE LESS." Because of the real audience this writing reached on *MySpace*, Tara spent a great deal of time intentionally crafting every element in this writing such as the symmetrical use of ellipses, the name of her favorite "BESTIE," and even her closing with the curt but child-like, "BYE." In Tara's construction of this writing nothing was a haphazard series of mistakes. There was a conscious and intentional effort towards grammar in Tara's writing. Tara also consciously attended to an audience through the embedded identities she constructed for herself as a best friend, an active adolescent, and a Christian. Yet, this type of writing is often trotted out as the culprit for adolescents' lowered aptitude with academic writing. More concerning to ponder than grammatical accuracy, however, are the deeper levels of identity performance in this writing. Tara positioned herself for anticipated criticism and gossip, but did she create an agentive identity for herself above the din of being a bully? Was Tara merely playing out female roles permissible to her (e.g., being a bestie)? Was her writing marked by social constraints? Did Tara's bold tone in her introduction give her a voice in this venue that prepared her for other more sophisticated digital venues? Or, was this tone merely another example of Tara picking a fight with her imagined and real "haters"?

There is no question information and communication technologies have changed the landscape of literacy. Even so, much of the girls' writing on *MySpace* was constructed and silenced by traditional ideologies for females. As such, what did access to ICTs mean for at-risk adolescent girls who stated they received no academic training in technology applications beyond word processing, power point, and Inspiration software in school, and were thus on their own to navigate participatory media in the rhetorically vast and peer-driven "co-apprenticeship" worlds of the Internet (Blake Yancey, 2009, p. 4)? In the wake of new literacies, perhaps a more useful question to ponder than whether ICTs ruined the girls' ability to produce academic writing would be to consider to what extent school literacy tasks prepared the girls for using ICTs in ways that would ensure their full civic participation in broader society.

New Literacies and Implications for Pedagogy

Routinely, I am asked my opinion about the extent to which adolescents' text messaging practices corrupt their writing in school. Working with adolescent girls who began to engage in texting and posting messages on *MySpace* during the course of the writing group, I was able to observe the girls' writing prior to and after such experiences. The girls who struggled with conventions of academic writing did so prior to their participation in online and digital forums. Those who had a better command of academic conventions for writing were better able to code switch between the two media just as many adults do who passed through adolescence prior to the dawn of the Internet and the Information Age. As such, I did not see evidence of text messaging language being a threat to the girls' success with academic writing. As Kiara stated, the girls may have needed to be reminded of the context for writing and made conscious of their use of text messaging language, but all of the girls code switched to the best of their ability when engaging in writing for school.

Beyond issues surrounding the mechanics of writing, more instruction for at-risk girls with a move towards social equity and critical interrogation of text is called for. Within the girls' arguably nascent use of information and communication technologies via the Internet rested the potential for learning more sophisticated literacy practices that would permit the girls to explore less restrictive identity performances. Thus, the girls needed instruction in critically framing literacy practices on the Internet.

The girls had overcome the digital divide in terms of access to technology. Using ICTs to forge agentive identities, however, was less evident. Their literacy identities and literacy practices were greatly shaped by the gender identities they adopted and constructed for themselves within the digital venues they explored. For instance, much of the text the girls generated on *MySpace* was filled with references to popular culture and celebrity fandom. Fandom also peppered the girls' writing and Discourse in the group. Lefstein and Snell (2011) cautioned that even though adolescents may be familiar with popular culture texts does not mean they have engaged with them beyond a superficial level of interpretation (p. 60). Alvermann and Hagood (2000) also viewed fandom as exerting a great deal of influence over adolescents' literacy practices. Alvermann and Hagood concluded fandom was "a window through which to view students' constructed identities" (p. 437) and a vehicle for critical media literacy.

Gounari (2009) referred to virtual spaces as sites for "public pedagogy" that consist of "a broader category beyond classroom practices, official curricula, and educational canons" (p. 148). Within this view of ICTs as occupying a hybridized formal and informal learning environment, Gounari argued that the evolution of literacy practices perpetually reproduces asymmetrical power relationships in which "people use their own reality and lived experiences as the basis for their evolving literacy" (p. 151). Similarly, Gonick (2007) noted, the Internet and social networking sites such as *MySpace* offer a "shifting media context where a proliferation of images of girls [exists] along with insistent incitements for them to speak," yet the ways girls are invited to dialogue remain restricted (p. 434). As such, girls in particular need instruction in resisting dominant and discriminatory ideologies and viewing the Internet "not as a technology but rather as a context in which to read, write, and communicate" (Leu, O'Bryne, Zawilinski, McVerry, & Everett-Cacopardo, 2009, p. 265).

Even with the push for higher levels of literacy in K-12 settings through educational policy mandates in the United States (e.g., No Child Left Behind), such initiatives remain predicated upon print-based notions of literacy and are largely removed from New Literacies practices. Also, the majority of state and national English language arts and reading standards created for analyzing print text are not tied to digital texts. Consequently, classroom teachers must construct pedagogy of their own volition that helps students "understand both the concept of ideology and how it relates to their own lives" in digital venues without any consistent guidelines for doing so (Gonick, 2007, p. 434). Referencing a similar concern about the lack of attention to New Literacies in policy mandates, Coiro, Knobel, Lankshear, and Leu (2008) noted,

> Unfortunately, the pervasive power of an assessment that only measures traditional print literacies profoundly determines what is taught during reading instruction, especially within schools that are under the greatest pressure to raise test scores. This has resulted in denying online reading experiences to students in the most economically challenged school districts. (p. 30)

In summary, schools are under a particular obligation to assist at-risk girls in learning to critically read the multitude of texts available to them online and to approach the Internet as an intellectual and social leveraging tool as writers.

Concluding Vignette: Seeking an Audience in Participatory Media

Although the girls were able to compose text with some multimodal features in the writing group, I have often wondered what would have happened if I had created a blog or wiki for the girls to participate in as part of the writing group. Would such media that could have been constructed separately from the built-in social architecture of *MySpace* have had as much appeal to the girls? Would they have engaged in writer's workshop more readily through a digital medium?

My graduate assistant and I created a *MySpace* page to interact with the girls outside of the group, but it was utilized only in a very limited fashion by the girls for sporadic e-mail exchanges with us and tagging photos we posted there. Even though we talked to the girls about engaging in more writing on *MySpace*, the girls explained repeatedly and unanimously their concerns about receiving criticism for what they wrote in such a shared, public space.

Isabel blogged two times on *MySpace* during the summer following her eighth grade year. Each blog was generated to express anger at a particular friend.

here I am in [name of a city] and I realized wat kinda frinds I had waiting for me but it's ok cuz now I know who is my friend n who is just a two fact lil bitch n I'm having a blast cuz I open my pretty brown eyes n I realized how much more potential I had so all I gotta say is it's wat eva bitch cuz I'm waitin for a how step up to me so she can get murkec on so duced nigha

In the follow-up blog posted a month later, Isabel wrote:

Gurls better look at tehm self b 4 you start bumpin yo gums and when you talk shit to some one please don't have yo mom or grandma beside you please cuz that's just childess already and gurls boo please grow up before you say you grown enough

Was Isabel's writing empowering? Was it a way for Isabel to begin to learn how to become a participatory citizen in a democracy? Although the blogs may have been read by the intended audience, each blog went unanswered and Isabel ceased to post any further writing on her blog.

References

Alvermann, D. (2010). *Adolescents' online literacies: Connecting classrooms, digital media & popular culture.* New York, NY: Peter Lang.

Alvermann, D., & Hagood, M. (2000). Fandom and critical media literacy. *Journal of Adolescent and Adult Literacy, 43* (5), 436–446.

Bean, T., Readance, J., & Baldwin, S. (2008). *Content area literacy: An integrated approach.* Dubuque, IA: Kendall/Hunt.

Beers, K. (2007). The measure of our success. In K. Beers, R. Probst, and L. Rief (Eds.), *Adolescent literacy: Turning promise into practice.* (pp. 1–14). Portsmouth, NH: Heinemann.

Blake Yancey, K. (2009). Writing in the 21st century. A Report from the National Council of Teachers of English. Retrieved June 2, 2011, from http://www.ncte.org/library/Files/Press/Yancey_final.pdf.

Bishop, N. (2008). *Frogs.* New York, NY: Scholastic Nonfiction.

Burke, J. (2007). Teaching English language arts in a "flat" world. In K. Beers, R. Probst, and L. Rief (Eds.), *Adolescent literacy: Turning promise into practice.* (pp. 149–166). Portsmouth, NH: Heinemann.

Coiro, J., Knobel, M., Lankshear, C., & Leu, D. (2008). Central issues in new literacies and new literacies research. In J. Coiro, M. Knobel, C. Lankshear, and D. Leu (Eds.), *Handbook of research on new literacies.* (pp. 1–63). New York, NY: Lawrence Erlbaum Associates.

Cope, B., & Kalantzis, M. (2009). "Multiliteracies": New literacies, new learning. *Pedagogies: An International Journal, 4,* 164–195.

Cullen, R. (2001). Addressing the digital divide. *Online Information Review, 25* (5), 311–320.

Gee, J. (2009). Reflections on reading cope and kalantzis' 'multiliteracies: New literacies, new learnings. *Pedagogies: An International Journal, 4,* 196–204.

Gonick, M. (2007). Girl number 20 revisited: Feminist literacies in new hard times. *Gender and Education, 19* (4), 433–454.

Gounari, P. (2009). Rethinking critical literacy in the new information age. *Critical Inquiry in Language Studies, 6* (3), 148–175.

Greenhow, C., Robelia, B., & Hughes, J. (2009). Learning, teaching and scholarship in a digital age: Web 2.0 and classroom research: What path should we take now? *Educational Researcher, 38* (4), 246–259.

Guzzetti, B., Elliott, K., & Welsch, D. (2010). *DIY media in the classroom: New literacies across content areas (middle through high school).* New York, NY: Teachers College Press.

Haas, C., Takayoshi, P., Carr, B., Hudson, K., & Pollock, R. (2011). Young people's everyday literacies: The language features of instant messaging. *Research in the Teaching of English, 45* (4), 378–404.

Hagood, M. (2009). *New literacies practices.* New York, NY: Peter Lang.

Hobbs, R. (2010). *Digital and media literacy: A plan for action.* Washington, DC: The Aspen Institute.

Knobel, M., & Lankshear, C. (2010). *DIY media: Creating, sharing, and learning with new technologies.* New York, NY: Peter Lang.

Lefstein, A., & Snell, J. (2011). Promises and problems of teaching with popular culture: A linguistic ethnographic analysis of discourse genre mixing in a literacy lesson. *Reading Research Quarterly, 46* (1), 40–69.

Leu, D., O'Bryne, W., Zawilinski, L., McVerry, G., & Everett-Cacopardo, H. (2009). Expanding the new literacies conversation. *Educational Researcher, 38* (4), 264–269.

Lewis, C., & Fabos, B. (2005). Instant messaging, literacies, and social identities. *Reading Research Quarterly, 40* (4), 470–501.

———. (2004). Digital literacies of the cybergirl. *E-Learning, 1* (3), 358–382.

New London Group. (2000). *Multiliteracies: Literacy learning and the design of social futures.* New York, NY: Routledge.

Street, B. (2003). What's 'new' in new literacy studies? Critical approaches to literacy in theory and practice. *Current Issues in Comparative Education,* 5 (2), 77—91.

Top French court declares internet access 'basic human right.'Times Online, Retrieved May 27, 2011 from http://technology.timesonline.co.uk/tol/news/tech_and_web/article 6478542.ece.

Thomas, A. (2007). *Youth online: Identity and literacy in the digital age.* New York, NY: Peter Lang.

Vigdor, J., & Ladd, H. (2010). Scaling the digital divide: Home computer technology and student achievement. Working Paper 48. Published by the National Center for Analysis of Longitudinal Data in Education Research.

Chapter Eight

Writing in the Third Space as a Way to Bring At-Risk Adolescent Girls out of the Periphery of School

Recently, Blake Yancey (2009), past president of NCTE, observed, "Through writing, we are" (p. 7). With this sentiment, Blake Yancey noted the power of writing to aid in human expression, reasoning, and connection to a larger grid of ideas. In the past two decades, there have been a multitude of books, policy reports, and studies devoted to the topic of teaching writing with similarly elegant theories. Yet, many students continue to fail to meet basic academic benchmarks in writing, and policy mandates fail to produce better means of prevention for such intellectual stagnation (The Institute for Education Sciences, 2007. Retrieved May 21, 2010 from http://www.nces.ed. gov/nationsreportcard/pdf/main2007/2009468.pdf). Somewhere in the midst of educational policy and classroom practice, at-risk adolescents remove themselves as much as possible from the equation of writing in school. But, what happens to such students whose writing potential becomes invisible within and beyond school? What happens to ethnic minority girls from low-income families whose public writing consists of a mass unconscious replication of language and identities in forums such as *MySpace* and whose private writing is never thoughtfully examined or cultivated? Without a bridge between their public and private writing practices, much of what at-risk adolescent girls could accomplish in both in-school and out-of-school settings is diminished. For the girls in this project, their public and private writing needed to be set in dialogue with one another in a space that allowed for both forms of writing to be encouraged and critically framed.

Creating a Bridge between In-School and Out-of-School Writing in the Third Space

Because the very nature of Third Space is one of hybridity, the writing group provided a forum where the worlds of public and private and in-school and out-of-school writing could coexist and become visible. The Third Space was also an important venue for this project because it afforded an opportunity to study adolescents engaged in voluntary writing practices. Guzzetti and Gamboa (2004) explained the importance of teachers developing an understanding of adolescents' voluntary literacy practices:

> It is important for teachers to become aware of how students use literacies to form and represent their identities, to construct meaning, and to pursue their own interests. If teachers can become aware of who their students really are, and what motivates them to read, and write, and learn how adolescents develop, practice, and refine their literacies outside of school, educators will be better equipped to connect those out-of-school literacy practices to the work students do in school. (p. 411)

The Third Space offered an opening for different kinds of text to move in and out of the setting, which allowed the girls' narratives to step out of the periphery of the school, however fleetingly. With such a fluid movement of texts, the Third Space also created a bridge between their out-of-school and in-school writing practices.

Donna Alvermann and her colleagues have written extensively about working with struggling youth in an after-school media club located in the quasi-school environment of a local public library (Alvermann, Hagood, Heron-Hruby, Hughes, Williams, & Yoon, 2007; Heron-Hruby, Hagood, & Alvermann, 2008). In this research, not only did the setting foster a hybrid between in-school and out-of-school literacy practices but also the roles the adults adopted were a hybrid between that of mentor, student, and teacher. In this type of context, adolescents provided adults with important windows into their uses of literacy and literacy identities. Heron-Hruby, Hagood, and Alvermann (2008) described the importance of the struggling adolescent readers having a voice in the types of texts they were permitted to read in the after-school setting. They argued giving adolescents a voice in discussion of what counts as text and what kinds of texts are permitted in school— especially popular culture texts—fosters an agentive transaction between the students and adults (e.g., teachers) the students encounter. Similar to these findings about sanctioned text, I discovered the importance of writing instruction that was supportive of multiple kinds of text, Discourse communities, vernacular language, and as generally non-judgmental as possible. The Third Space writing setting predicated upon disrupted roles of adults and students helped facilitate this environment.

Creating a bridge between girls' in-school and out-of-school literacies is important because, as Grote (2006) contended, teachers need "to know what adolescents can already do with literacy" and "vernacular literacies embrace the local knowledges valued by community members" (pp. 478–479). Further, the Third Space supports at-risk adolescent girls' writing through "challenging the boundaries between official and vernacular literacies" (p. 478).

By the end of three years of participation in the writing group, Isabel composed a narrative about her day that began with the sentence, "I woke up dismorning and I felt find but once I took a bath my stomach started hurting." After completing a paragraph Isabel called me over to read her writing and asked me whether she should quote her mom again in her story and what else she should do to "fix" her writing. Seeing that the word "dismorning" was underlined in red to denote a spelling error, I asked Isabel if she wanted to separate "dis" from "morning" in her writing. She looked at me puzzled and said, "But it's a word." I responded, "Is it a word you hear your friends use?"

"Yeah. But everybody uses this word at school," Isabel reasoned.

"Oh, like 'How are you dismorning?'" I asked.

"Yeah."

This exchange prompted a discussion between all of the girls in attendance during that day and myself about vernacular language, slang, and written language. I explained that in academic writing, these words would be written as "this morning" and emphasized that one register for language was not better than the other, just dependent on a particular social context. After this discussion, Isabel revised the first sentence in her narrative to, "I woke up this morning and I felt fine but once I took a bath my stomach started hurting."

The Third Space as Critical Literacy

Virtually all of the girls evolved in their writing to present more agentive personas about themselves as writers within the group. When I asked Kecia what she had learned through her participation in the writing group, she stated matter-of-factly that she never thought she could write before. Other spaces or contexts for literacy did not present the same evidence. Thus, a Third Space setting where identities and literacies could be "made and re-made over time" was vital (Wissman, 2011, p. 410). In the Third Space Tara could stop being a bully, Felicia could process her relationship with her mother, Isabel could trust an audience with her writing, Kecia could examine sexual harassment, Kiara could confide a secret, Veronica could confront racism, and Amber could change her mind about the futility of her life. In the Third Space at-risk adolescent girls could rename their lived experiences and construct a new literacy identity. Amber summed up her transformation through writing about her lived experiences in the group in the final piece she wrote in the project:

Change

Sometimes change is good. Sometimes it helps like I use to want to kill myself, but I knew I had to change. But know day by day, hour by hour, and minute by minute. I'm getting better. I'm not so crazy. But its just change that helped me. Some people might think change is bad but I know It is the best thing.

After writing about devastating lived experiences in previous narratives, Amber crafted this piece on a change in her outlook. In this writing, Amber situated herself as the agent of significant change in her life. The statements "I'm getting better" and "I'm not so crazy" demonstrated Amber's growing awareness of her ability to re-invent herself in her narrative. In the Third Space, Amber used writing to "name and intervene in experiences often repressed or denied" (Wissman, 2011, p. 421). In doing so, Amber constructed a new, empowered narrative identity for herself from previous narrative identities where she defined her value through molestation and the ways boys viewed her. Could Amber have reached this insight without a space undergirded by a philosophy of critical literacy?

Lankshear and Knobel (2009) described critical literacy as "powerful literacy" consisting of "practices that identify and critique Discourses that regulate who and what we become individually and collectively" (p. 72). Although adopting a critical literacy philosophy does not always mean an immediate metamorphosis for students (e.g., Ellsworth, 1989; Ralfe, 2009), the ultimate goal is one of liberation through awareness and transformation of status quo, oppressive Discourse. A philosophy of critical literacy swirled around the context of the writing group through the opening up of a space where the girls were free to write about their lived experiences in numerous and shifting social registers. The girls' daily experiences with sexual harassment, racism, and the expectations of stereotypic heterosexual gender roles were hegemonic narratives the girls collectively—and in most instances individually—had not named as such prior to participating in the writing group. Critical literacy as an examination of ideology, representation, omission of perspectives in socially privileged texts, and a call to action emerged slowly in the group but eventually started to take root through the girls' writing about social injustice. Much of the girls' private writing in hidden journals at home talked back to the oppression they felt, but this writing was effectively silenced as a series of vanquished, infuriated notations. As the girls realized they had an audience for these narratives in the Third Space, they began to use this forum to cross between their private and public selves. Through such crossings, the girls fundamentally shaped the Third Space writing group. While there were plenty of moments of jocularity, fandom, and even fighting in the writing group, there were also profoundly intense moments of introspection, confession, acceptance, and an emergence of liberatory writing. Thus, the Third Space was key to fostering critical literacy.

How Can Schools Meet the Literacy Needs of At-Risk Adolescent Girls?

Years ago, when I was teaching a professional development seminar to elementary teachers in West Philadelphia, a third grade teacher admitted unapologetically, "My students can't even write a complete paragraph, so I don't teach writing." Since this experience, I have heard several similar confessions from teachers about their use of "teach around" methods for students who "cannot write." By the same token, I have observed numerous students begrudgingly carve words on paper and resist writing altogether in school settings. Both of these scenarios capture the mutual helplessness students and teachers often feel towards the prospect of teaching and learning to write.

At the end of their last year in the writing group, I asked Amber and Isabel what kind of writing instruction they wanted to receive in high school, to which they offered the following advice:

ML: So, when you think about going to high school, what kind of writing instruction would be ideal?

Isabel: I would like a class at [name of the high school] where they let you write on a computer for a whole period. Tell you what you need to write and then leave you alone. If you need help then you will raise your hand. Other than that just leave you alone. Let us write. Because if I have a teacher all upon me, I don't want you to come and sit down and correct me. I want to write what I want to write and then you can correct me at the end. . . . I need space.

Amber: So, you don't want them all up in your business. Please can you just wait til I'm finished?

Isabel: I thought it was mine, not yours!

Through this discussion Isabel and Amber addressed their need to feel a sense of autonomy about their writing. Isabel and Amber had a highly independent view of writing in terms of the process of composing text. They also did not want to be interrupted or monitored by a teacher in the midst of composing. This discussion also hinted at the importance of allowing space for girls' narratives within the writing curriculum.

Beyond this advice, through this project I learned of the importance of encouraging nascent writing, the need for constancy with practicing writing that may never be read, and staving off criticism until students feel accepted as writers. Even so, the most important pedagogical element I learned through this experience was the need for schools to create spaces for at-risk adolescent girls' narratives. To this end, I feel educators need to consider two fundamental components in their work with at-risk adolescent girls: (1) how the narratives of adolescent girls are represented or situated in schools, and (2) how the curriculum fosters/acknowledges/makes space for such narratives.

Finding an Uneasy Closure to Our Work Together: Looking Ahead

Veronica sent me an email on *MySpace* recently:

> Hello, I am doing just amazing. I am now a sophomore and time is passing by so fast. I am on the [high school] Junior Varsity team, and I am still singing in choir. Yes I am writing still, it sure does come in handy in English AP. I now have over 60 pages of poems that I have worked on. How are you guys doing? Who is now in the writing group? Hopefully soon, I can go over and meet some of the kids. I get to leave campus now, so it's pretty amazing. Well I hope to hear some great things from the new writers, and I soon hope to meet some of the new members. Please keep in touch.

As I write the final words for this book, I can report that the girls highlighted throughout each chapter are still in high school, still corresponding with me on occasion via e-mail, and still aware that I am interested in their success although I no longer see them on a weekly basis. Even though a day rarely passes that I do not think of the girls and worry about their futures beyond high school, I hope somewhere in their collection of middle school memories they always carry an image of me sitting next to them, smiling at their giddy displays of fandom, calmly absorbing their secrets, and telling them as they paused in the midst of composing to seek my feedback, "Good. Keep going."

References

Alvermann, D., Hagood, M., Heron-Hruby, A., Hughes, P., Williams, K., & Yoon, J. (2007). Telling themselves who they are: What one out-of-school time study revealed about underachieving readers. *Reading Psychology, 28,* 31–50.

Blake Yancey, K. (2009). Writing in the 21st century. A Report from the National Council of Teachers of English. Retrieved June 2, 2011 from http://www.ncte.org/library/Files/Press /Yancey_final.pdf.

Ellsworth, E. (1989). Why doesn't this feel empowering? Working through the repressive myths of critical pedagogy. *Harvard Educational Review, 59* (3), 279–325.

Grote, E. (2006). Challenging the boundaries between school-sposored and venacular literacies: Urban indigenous teenage girls writing in an "at risk" programme. *Language and Education, 20* (6), 478–492.

Guzzetti, B., & Gamboa, M. (2004). Zines for social justice: Adolescent girls writing on their own. *Reading Research Quarterly, 39* (4), 408–436.

Heron-Hruby, A., Hagood, M., & Alvermann, D. (2008). Switching places and looking to adolescents for the practices that shape school literacies. *Reading & Writing Quarterly, 24,* 311–334.

Institute of Education Sciences . (2010). The nation's report card: Writing 2007. Author. Retrieved May 21, 2010 from http://nces.ed.gov/nationsreportcard/pdf/main2007/ 2009468.pdf.

Lankshear, C., & Knobel, M. (2009). More than words: Chris Searle's approach to critical literacy as cultural action. *Race & Class, 51* (2), 59–78.

Ralfe, E. (2009). Policy: Powerful or pointless? An exploration of the role of critical literacy in challenging and changing gender stereotypes. *Language Learning Journal, 37* (3), 305–321.

Wissman, K. (2011). "Rise up!": Literacies, lived experiences, and identities within an in-school "other space." *Research in the Teaching of Writing, 45* (4), 405–438.

Appendix A

Research Methodology

Methodologically, this study was grounded in socio-cultural literacy theories (Gee, 2005; Haas Dyson, 2004; Heath, 2004). Methods of data collection constitute a qualitative research project (Erickson, 1986) predicated upon a practitioner research stance (Bauman & Duffy-Hester, 2002). To guide this project, I developed the following research questions:

1. What happens when "at-risk" adolescent girls participate in a writing group situated within the context of a Third Space intervention program?
2. How do the adolescent girls compose texts within this setting (e.g., rehearse, peer edit, revise)?
3. What kinds of Discourse communities (Gee, 2005) are evident in the girls' writing?
4. What kinds of Discourse models (Gee, 2005) do the girls hold about writing?
5. How do the girls interact with one another around writing within the group setting?
6. What kinds of audiences do the girls attend to as writers?
7. What role does technology play in composing texts for the girls?
8. How do the girls construct narratives that forge and assert identities?
9. What tropes and genres dominate the narratives in their writing?
10. In what ways are literacy identities expressed against the backdrop of narratives about their gender and ethnicity?

Data Sources

Data sources for this study included: participant-observation analytic field notes (Spradley, 1980) of weekly writing group sessions, transcriptions of the literacy group sessions, semi-structured interviews conducted with the participants in the study (Seidman, 2006), periodic informal interviews with a key informant in the middle school setting (Carspecken, 1996), a collection of student writing samples of both prompted and unprompted writing generated during the writing group as well as writings the participants shared spontaneously as representative of other venues for literacy (Mahiri, 2003) (e.g., school assignments, personal writing, and *MySpace* entries), and a reflective journal of each weekly session I kept.

Data Analysis

I analyzed data for this study through coding all of the data sources for themes (Harry, Sturges, & Klingner, 2005); conducting discourse analysis (Gee, 2005) over key passages in the transcripts of the literacy group sessions, the interviews, and the archive of student writing gathered in the study, and engaging in narrative inquiry (Ellis, 2004). I began data analysis through recording open codes over the transcripts, student writings, and my reflective journal and then refining these codes into axial codes, which consisted of combining codes with similar patterns. Finally, I established predominant themes or theoretical codes from the axial codes. To deepen my understanding of these themes, I conducted discourse analysis over excerpts from the transcripts and student writings that I identified as exemplifying both typical and significant patterns in the data to help me gain greater insights into the girls' cultural models for writing and narrative identities.

I relied on Gee's (2005) seven building tasks to guide the discourse analysis. Gee's building tasks include the categories of significance, activities, identities, relationships, politics, connections, and sign systems and knowledge (pp. 11–13). To verify analysis of the writing group sessions, I conducted interviews with nine of the girls participating in the group. In these interviews, I asked the girls about their views of the group and their experiences as writers both within and outside of the group. I also engaged in member checking of the major themes I had discovered through preliminary data analysis of the transcripts, reflective researcher's journal, and student writing. Through all of this data analysis, I hoped to better understand the girls' perspectives about their processes of writing and literacy identities within this setting. The following themes emerging from the data analysis became the basis for the chapters in this book:

1. Perceived Audiences for Self-Initiated Writing
2. Exerting Power and Control within the Discourse of the Group and within Writing
3. The Dichotomy of School and Nonschool Cultural Models of Writing
4. Writing as a Mirror for Identities
5. Writing as a Form of Agency for Social Disparities with Ethnic and Gender References
6. Tropes and Narratives about Anger in Writing
7. Sexualized Identities and Gender Roles Expressed in Writing

References

Bauman, J., & Duffy-Hester, A. (2002). Making sense of classroom worlds: Methodology in teacher research. In M. Kamil, P. Mosenthal, P. D. Pearson, and R. Barr (Eds.), *Methods of literacy research: The methodology chapters from the handbook of reading research,* Vol. 3. (pp. 1–22). Mahwah, NJ: Lawrence Erlbaum Associates.

Carspecken, P. (1996). Critical ethnography in educational research: A theoretical and practical guide. New York: Routledge.

Ellis, C. (2004). *The ethnographic I: A methodological novel about autoethnography.* New York: Alta Mira Press.

Erickson, F. (1986). Qualitative methods in research on teaching. In M. C. Wittrock (Ed.), *Handbook of research on teaching,* 3rd ed. (pp.119–161). New York: Macmillan Publishing Company.

Gee, J. (2005). *An introduction to discourse analysis theory and method.* New York: Routledge.

Haas Dyson, A. (2004). Writing and the sea of voices: Oral language in, around, and about writing. In R. Ruddell and N. Unrau (Eds.), *Theoretical models and processes of reading.* (pp. 146–162). Newark, DE; International Reading Association.

Harry, B., Sturges, K., & Klingner, J. (2005). Mapping the process: An exemplar of process and challenges in grounded theory analysis. *Educational Researcher, 34* (2), 3–13.

Heath, S. B. (2004). The children of trackton's children: Spoken and written language in social change. In R. Ruddell and N. Unrau (Eds.), *Theoretical models and processes of reading.* (pp. 187–209). Newark, DE; International Reading Association.

Mahiri, J. (2004). *What they don't learn in school: Literacy in the lives of urban youth.* New York, NY: Peter Lang Publishers.

Seidman, I. (2006). *Interviewing as qualitative research: A guide for researchers in education and the social sciences.* New York: Teachers College Press.

Spradley, J. (1980). *Participant observation.* New York: Harcourt Brace Jovanovich.

Appendix B

Texas College and Career Readiness Standards for Writing

A. Compose a variety of texts that demonstrate clear focus, the logical development of ideas in well-organized paragraphs, and the use of appropriate language that advances the author's purpose.

1. Determine effective approaches, forms, and rhetorical techniques that demonstrate understanding of the writer's purpose and audience.
2. Generate ideas and gather information relevant to the topic and purpose, keeping careful records of outside sources.
3. Evaluate relevance, quality, sufficiency, and depth of preliminary ideas and information, organize material generated, and formulate a thesis.
4. Recognize the importance of revision as the key to effective writing. Each draft should refine key ideas and organize them more logically and fluidly, use language more precisely and effectively, and draw the reader to the author's purpose.
5. Edit writing for proper voice, tense, and syntax, assuring that it conforms to standard English, when appropriate. (p. 3)

Author Index

Subject Index

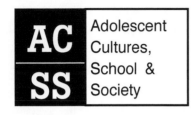

Adolescent
Cultures,
School &
Society

Joseph L. DeVitis & Linda Irwin-
DeVitis
GENERAL EDITORS

As schools struggle to redefine and restructure themselves, they need to be aware of the new realities of adolescents. Thus, this series of monographs and texts is committed to depicting the variety of adolescent cultures that exist in today's troubled world. It is primarily a qualitative research, practice, and policy series devoted to contextual interpretation and analysis that encompasses a broad range of interdisciplinary critique. In addition, this series seeks to address issues of curriculum theory and practice; multicultural education; aggression, bullying, and violence; the media and arts; school dropouts; homeless and runaway youth; gangs and other alienated youth; at-risk adolescent populations; family structures and parental involvement; and race, ethnicity, class, and gender/LGBTQ studies.

Send proposals and manuscripts to the general editors at:
Joseph L. DeVitis & Linda Irwin-DeVitis
Darden College of Education
Old Dominion University
Norfolk, VA 23503

To order other books in this series, please contact our Customer Service Department at:
(800) 770-LANG (within the U.S.)
(212) 647-7706 (outside the U.S.)
(212) 647-7707 FAX

or browse online by series at:
WWW.PETERLANG.COM